Curds & Whey

Susan Ogilvy

Illustrated by Juliet Stanwell Smith

B.T. Batsford Ltd London

Acknowledgment

I would like to thank the following:

Elizabeth Buckley for her invaluable help with initial research whilst I was still living in Africa. Kathleen Tucker, my aunt, who gave me her copy of Elizabeth Raffald's *The Experienced English Housekeeper* which had been handed down to her, and is now a treasured possession. The staff of the British Museum and the Guildhall libraries who allowed me access to the old cookery books. Carol Clarke of the Milk Marketing Board for advice over metrication of the recipes. My long-suffering family who ate and approved most of the recipes in this book, and more besides.

For my mother, Betty Christmas

Printed in Great Britain by
The Anchor Press Ltd
Tiptree, Essex
for the publishers
B.T. Batsford Ltd
4 Fitzhardinge Street
London W1H 0AH

Contents

Preface

The esteemed Mrs Beeton in her *Book of Household Management* remarked:

From no other substance, solid or fluid, can so great a number of distinct kinds of aliment be prepared as from milk; some forming food, others drink; some of them delicious, and deserving the name of luxuries; all of them wholesome, and some medicinal: indeed, the variety of aliments that seems capable of being produced from milk, appears to be quite endless. In every age this must have been a subject for experiment, and every nation has added to the number by the invention of some peculiarity of its own.

This was written in 1861, and is still as true today as it has been through the ages. In this book I have attempted to collect some of the old and traditional English recipes and methods used for making these foods and dishes, of both the luxurious and the wholesome, plainer kinds.

The book will appeal to those who have their own supply of milk be it from a dairy herd, a house cow or goat and wish to make their own basic ingredients for the recipes: the cream and butter, cheese and yoghurt or just curds and whey. Those who do not own cows or goats are not precluded: soft cheeses, yoghurt, curds and whey can be made inexpensively at home from milk bought from the dairy or shop. It is not impossible to separate cream or make butter in small quantities from bought milk if so wished, although it is more worthwhile if you have a larger supply of milk available. Many of the milk products besides milk can be bought of course: soft curd or lactic cheese, cream cheese and skimmed milk are available in grocery shops and supermarkets as well as an infinite variety of other cheeses, yoghurts and creams of varying butterfat content for different purposes.

The traditional recipes come to us from old recipe books and manuscripts, from *The Forme of Cury*, an ancient fourteenth century manuscript, to Mrs Beeton herself. As you read through these old cookery books you can see how the recipe for a particular dish has changed through the centuries. Many of our recipes in common use now are really very old recipes which have been adapted beyond recognition and often for the worse, so that it is a delicious surprise to go back to the original recipe and find out how good the dish can be. This applies particularly to many of the milk-based recipes: the custards and trifles, the soups and sauces, the mousses and bread puddings, the possets and syllabubs.

Along with traditional recipes I have included a few modern, especially yoghurt-based recipes, for yoghurt is a recent addition to our diet although sour milk has been used in various forms for a long time. Many of the recipes using yoghurt are Middle Eastern in origin, not unnaturally, as this is the home of yoghurt. This is not an unusual source as many of our traditional recipes were brought back originally from the Middle East by the Crusaders. It is perhaps surprising that yoghurt itself was not introduced to England at that time as well.

Some of the old recipes have been adapted according to modern needs and pockets. We no longer require to take a dozen eggs, three pounds of flour or 2 pints of cream for a given recipe; our families are not so large, eggs are bigger than they were then, we are more diet conscious. I hope you will enjoy your 'experiments' with milk and using its products in these recipes, both ancient and modern. I am sure that you will come to agree with Mrs Beeton.

1 The history of milk in British cookery

In Britain milk has played a part in the diet since the time of the Neolithic farmers who milked cows, goats and sheep. Containers made from leather, porous pottery or even wood were used, which must have been difficult to clean; most milk must have soured very quickly and so was consumed in that condition. Remains of perforated colanders found on Bronze Age sites indicate that simple soft cheeses may have been made at this time, the colanders used to drain the whey. It is thought that butter making was introduced by the Celts, and that they used salt to preserve it.

The Romans most certainly introduced more sophisticated ways of making cheese in which rennet was used to clot the warm milk. The curd was drained in baskets or moulds with weights to press out the whey. It was salted and further allowed to dry outdoors, then stored indoors and left to mature. This process produced a hard cheese, very similar in its manufacture to the hard cheeses of today. Such a cheese has less moisture than the soft cheeses drained by gravity, and it develops flavour and texture as it matures, and keeps for much longer.

The Romans also used cheese in their cookery. Hard cheese formed part of salads, soft curd cheese was put into complicated *patina* dishes with many other ingredients, or was used as a substitute for butter in cakes or pastries. In Britain butter and lard were likely to be the main cooking fats.

After the Romans left, the invading Angles, Saxons and Danes introduced new food habits to England. The Saxons made milk puddings with barley, oats and honey; there were cheeses and oatcakes. The Danes who were good farmers introduced new skills such as methods for storing butter and cheese. One Danish custom was that of eating fish with milk, and meat with ale on alternate days.

In early medieval times Englishmen of all classes enjoyed the 'white meats', as milk and milk products were called, but by the sixteenth century they were considered as food for the poor. Indeed the peasant's cow provided him with butter, cheese, curds, whey, cream, raw milk, sour milk and buttermilk, and his diet must have consisted mainly of these products and bread. Langland's immortal Piers Plowman laments:

I have no penny
to buy pullets, nor geese, nor pigs,
but I have two green cheeses,
a few curds and cream,
an oatcake,
two loaves of beans and bran baked for my children.

The rich man was essentially a meat eater, but even so milk and milk products were used in cookery and were a useful addition to his diet. The cream was skimmed off, some to be made into best quality butter, some to be eaten raw. Rich custards and custard tarts of fifteenth century recipes were made with cream. The skimmed milk was used for cheese making.

Whey and buttermilk, by-products of cheese and buttermaking were drunk fresh or could be made into curds which were eaten with honey, cream, ale or wine. Curds were used in tarts and were made into fritters.

There were three types of cheese: the hard cheese made from skimmed milk which was the peasants' staple, soft cheese from whole or semi-skimmed milk which matured for a time but still had enough moisture to be soft, and the new or green cheese which had to be eaten within a few days as it contained much moisture. The full cream milk cheese or 'rowene' was the one eaten by the rich, and used in cheese tarts. Herbs were added to the soft curd cheese which was given the name of 'spermyse'. There were regional hard cheeses, cheese was even imported from Holland and Normandy.

Butter was made in a tall churn with a wooden plunger which was pulled up and down to agitate the cream. Sweet butter was beaten in fresh water until free of buttermilk and then slightly salted; salt butter was made by pressing out the buttermilk by hand alone and then salting heavily for keeping. For cooking purposes butter was clarified, that is to say, melted, strained and put into pots.

Both cows and sheep were milked – in the Yorkshire dales local cheeses were made from ewes' milk from the large monastery flocks; in the south of England the cow was more common. Gradually the cow took over as the main supplier of milk.

In the seventeenth century enclosure began and it had an effect on the former 'white meat' diet of the poor. Few could afford to keep a cow now: there were larger herds of cows but these were kept by the big landowners. The milk was turned into cheese and butter and sold in markets or sent to the large towns, some of the whey and buttermilk was also sold, so little now reached the country labourer. He had a little cheese and butter and that was all. The situation was better for those in the north as there was more open grazing land and small farmers sold their milk locally.

On the other hand the rich began to use more milk, cream and butter in their cooking. Milk was used in the new drinks such as drinking chocolate, and later added to tea and coffee. Little milk was drunk as such, but whey was very popular and it was thought to be more wholesome than milk. Cream and milk were mixed with spiced and sweetened wine and ale to give rich syllabubs and posset drinks.

Cream was used liberally in all cookery, and especially in the rich 'banquet' dessert sweets which were served at the end of the meal to tempt the fading appetite. These included the trifles, fools, flummeries, creams, snows, junkets and tipsy cakes so well enjoyed in Tudor and Stuart times and later. Clotted cream was made by leaving new milk in shallow bowls over a low heat for some hours. It was eaten with sugar or with fresh cream.

Ice cream was first made in the eighteenth century. At first plain or sweetened cream was frozen but later recipes were developed which used sieved fruit or jam mixed together with sugar and cream. The ice cream was made in special basins, with an inner basin to hold the cream mixture and an outer one to hold the ice. The cream was removed from the ice every so often and beaten to prevent the formation of large ice crystals in the mixture and so give a smooth, even texture.

Curds were still used in cookery especially in curd tarts or cheesecakes as they were called, but cheese was becoming more important. Local cheese varieties were better known than before and were sold at special markets or cheese fairs. The methods of making them varied in different parts of the country, and the soil type influenced the flavour and texture of the cheese. During this time Cheshire, Cheddar, Single and Double Gloucester, Blue Vinney of Dorset and Stilton all acquired a national reputation.

In the summer soft curd cheeses were made, they were often coloured and flavoured with marigold, spinach or sage juice and served at the banquet course. But the hard mature cheese was the every day cheese, eaten at the end of the meal as today. It was cooked in cheese omelettes, toasted as 'Welsh Rabbit' (nowadays, Welsh Rarebit) and potted with butter and wine.

In the eighteenth century the horizontal barrel churn with paddles superseded the medieval upright churn. Butter, made from the milk of the fresh summer grass, was rich and golden. It became usual to colour the paler butters such as winter or whey butter with marigold or carrot juice to imitate the summer colour. Butter was sold in the special butter markets built of stone so that the produce remained cold, or sent by sea, road or canal to the larger towns.

Bread and butter was the poor man's breakfast while toasted bread or wiggs (spiced and sweetened buns) spread with butter were eaten by the middle classes for breakfast and afternoon tea. Butter was used ubiquitously in cookery not only for cakes and pastry, for frying and basting but it was also 'run over' salads, vegetables, meat stews and fish.

The nineteenth century saw the development of industrialization not least in the dairy industry, and the beginning of scientific methods applied to agriculture. But until well after the middle of the century the quality of milk supplied in towns was very bad, often watered, skimmed of fat and a potent carrier of disease and infection. It was not until the very end of the century that the discovery of pasteurization could ensure protection against milk-borne disease.

Condensed and dried milk began to be made and condensed skimmed milk which was a cheap by-product of the butter factories, was commonly used for feeding young children mostly in the large industrial towns. Margarines were formulated and manufactured as a cheap substitute for butter; thus mass production of manufactured food began.

Nowadays there is a swing back to the so-called simple life of self-sufficiency and home production, even if we cannot do without our modern deep freeze or food mixer. Nevertheless there is a wish to produce foods and dishes from the basic raw materials rather than buy the convenient package, and perhaps even to grow or produce these raw materials at home.

Milk and its products still remain an important part of our diet. Quite apart from forming an essential ingredient of so many varied recipes, the diet would be poorer nutritionally without milk. It is still one of our best and most economical protein foods and an excellent source of calcium. For children it is an essential food for healthy growth; even if they do not like milk to drink, they will generally enthuse over fruit yoghurts, ice creams, chocolate pudding with sauce and especially milk shakes. Milk provides older people with ready and convenient nourishment, and can be used in soups and desserts which are light and easy to eat. For vegetarians, milk and other dairy products help balance the diet. It would be difficult to find a better food. Of course there may be those who are concerned with overweight or with too much fat in their diet. Milk should be part of a slimming diet because of the essential nutrients it contains; it must be remembered that all foods are fattening if taken in excess and a slimming diet should be well balanced with all foods taken in moderation. Those who wish to avoid the fat can skim their milk and leave the cream for others; excellent yoghurt, soft cheeses and even milk ices can be made from skimmed milk. In some of the recipes it is possible to substitute single cream for double cream, milk for single cream, skimmed milk for milk, if a less rich dish is required. There is certainly room to experiment in your milk cookery.

2 Making your own dairy products

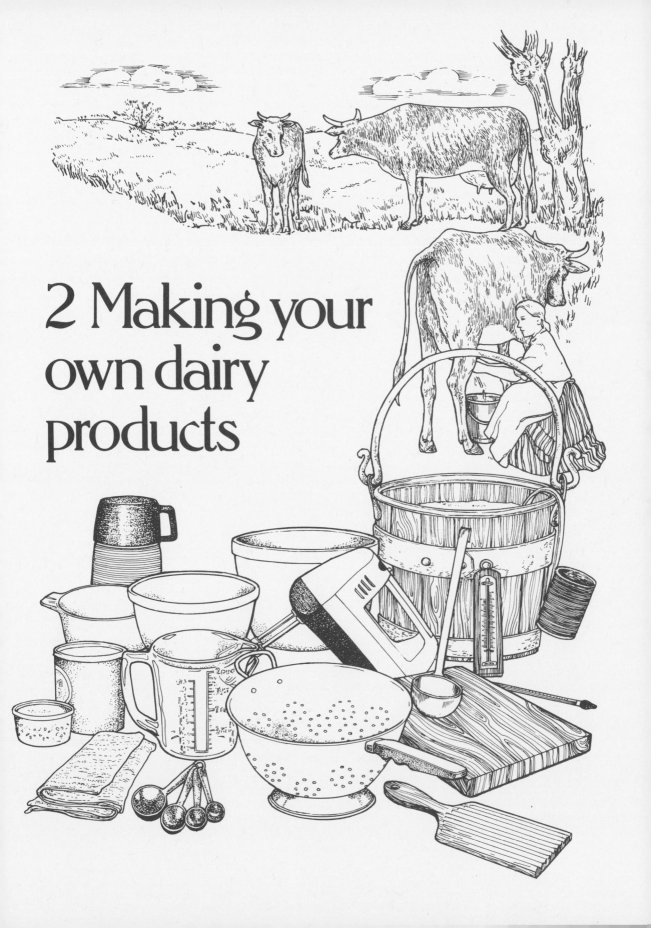

First of all it is helpful to understand why we can make so many different dairy foods from milk, and so I have included a brief description of the composition of milk and its properties.

The structure of milk

Milk is an interesting substance. It is produced by all mammals for their young and as such is a complete food providing for all their nutritional needs. Its composition of course varies according to the growth rate and needs of the species: cow's milk varies considerably from human, because the growth of the calf is obviously so much greater than that of the human baby. Milk is a complex mixture of proteins, fat, sugar and water together with minerals and vitamins, and it is the properties of these constituents which enable so many different products to be made from milk.

The main protein in milk is called casein. This exists as suspended particles combined with the mineral calcium. When the milk becomes very acid or rennet is added, these particles separate out and the milk becomes junket-like in consistency, forming a curd. This is known as coagulation or clotting. Rennet is a substance found in the stomach of young mammals and it enables their milk to form a clot so that it can be easily digested. We extract this rennet for making cheese.

The curd which is first formed holds much liquid known as whey, and to make cheese, much of this whey must be removed. The processes by which it is removed and how much is removed will depend on the type of cheese to be made; for example, more whey is removed from a hard cheese than a soft cheese.

Two types of curd are formed: the rennet curd and the acid curd. Rennet curd is the basis of most hard and soft cheeses. Acid curd is used for acid curd cheeses, yoghurt and other cultured milk products. It is formed when a high acidity develops in the milk. Raw untreated milk will sour or become more acid naturally, because it contains a number of beneficial milk-loving bacteria. These bacteria use the milk sugar, called lactose, for growth and in so doing ferment it to lactic acid. Obviously this occurs more quickly if milk is left in warm conditions favourable to their growth; after a time it will be noticed that the milk has clotted.

Most of the milk we drink now in the UK is pasteurized to make it absolutely safe. Pasteurization kills all the disease organisms and also most of the lactic acid producing bacteria, so improving its keeping quality. Even if you have a supply of raw milk from the farm it is advisable to pasteurize it since you never know what disease organisms may be present. So with pasteurized milk a special culture of lactic acid producing bacteria must be used to start the souring process. There are many different types of lactic bacteria, and the culture used depends on the product to be made.

Even when making cheese with rennet, a bacterial culture is used.

Rennet works best when the milk is slightly acid and also warm (not boiled or very hot when it will not work at all). The acidity continues to develop after the curd has formed and helps to give cheese its flavour and also acts as a preservative. The cultures used in cheese making are known as cheese 'starters'.

When making yoghurt, a yoghurt culture is used. This contains a mixture of bacteria which give yoghurt its special flavour.

The fat in milk consists of many tiny fat particles or globules, each surrounded by a very thin layer of protein. This layer of protein enables the fat to exist as an emulsion in the watery liquid of milk and so be easily digested by young animals. The fat particles are lighter than the rest of the milk and so rise to the surface, forming a cream layer. It can be separated easily from the rest of the milk; cream still contains some water and other milk constituents, together with the fat. The fat globules remain separate even in the cream layer. You can see this when you shake a bottle of milk because the cream is quickly redistributed throughout the milk. Homogenized milk has no cream layer, for in this process the fat globules are broken down to very small particles and they remain evenly distributed throughout the milk; the friction is so great on the larger surface area per volume of each globule that it cannot rise. Similarly the fat globules in goat's milk are much smaller than those of cow's milk and the cream layer takes much longer to rise. The fat in homogenized milk and goat's milk is easily digested because of the smaller particle size and so they are suitable for young babies or children who have difficulty in digesting the fat.

To make butter the protein layers surrounding the fat globules must be broken to release the fat. This is achieved by churning, the action breaks the layers and the fat inside merges together to form butter granules which separate from the liquid portion, the buttermilk.

Equipment and ingredients

It is comparatively easy to make your own dairy products at home and for most of these products used in the recipes in this book, no special equipment is needed beyond that which you would have in your kitchen already. It includes the following:

a thermometer – an ordinary jam- making thermometer can be used. There
  is a special dairy thermometer which floats in the liquid but it is fairly
  expensive
a room thermometer, to check the temperature of places used to incubate
  yoghurt
a 1 litre (2 pt) graduated measuring jug
heatproof mixing bowls of varying sizes; these can be pyrex or plastic, the
  latter have fitted lids which are useful

butter muslin (for draining cheese)
stainless steel spoons, ladles and knives
set of plastic measuring spoons
plastic sieve or colander
old plastic food containers such as margarine and ice cream tubs, yoghurt
 and cream cartons to make into moulds and containers
wide-necked thermos flask (for incubating yoghurt)
large, shallow pan or bowl (for cream separation)
hand skimmer or thin-edged saucer (for cream separation)
small hand or electric churn, or hand or electric beater (for butter)
scotch hands or wooden spoons (for butter)
small wooden or formica board (for butter)
sterilization liquid or tablets

Milk is a very good growth medium for bacteria, both beneficial and
harmful. Because it can be easily contaminated by harmful bacteria, it is
essential to take great care in cleaning and sterilization of all equipment
used in making dairy products.

After use, rinse and scrub the utensils in cold water first to remove milk
deposits. Then wash and scrub in hot soapy water, using an ordinary
kitchen detergent. For wooden, butter-making equipment use washing
soda crystals as detergent makes the wood sticky and could taint the
butter. Then rinse thoroughly in clean hot water and place in a sterilizing
solution. This can be made up in the same way as for baby bottles;
sterilizing liquid or tablets are easily available at chemists. Metal, other
than stainless steel, should not be put in the solution as it can be corroded,
but can be boiled. Muslin cloths need special care as their very nature
makes them a good harbouring ground for bacteria; rinse well in cold water
and remove all adhering particles, then wash in hot soapy water and
finally sterilize in the solution or boil. Rinse the equipment in clean cold
water, leave to drain dry and store in a clean dry place. Sterilize again
before use.

The list of ingredients needed is very small:

milk, preferably pasteurized. Sterilized or ultra-heat-treated (Long Life)
 milks can be used for making yoghurt
junket rennet tablets or rennet essence, available from health food and
 grocery shops
household salt
fresh yoghurt. Check the date code – there should be at least a week left
 before it expires. The caps should be tight and not 'blown'; buy from
 chilled cabinets only
dried, skimmed milk powder

Milk pasteurization at home

Whether your milk comes direct from the farm or you buy it, it is advisable to use pasteurized milk so that you are sure that it is absolutely safe. It is a relatively simple and quick process once you have established a routine for your own supplies.

Pour the milk into a heatproof container, a stainless steel bucket or bowl, pyrex or heatproof plastic bowl, and then place this container in a large pan filled with water so that the level of the water is level with the milk in its container. Place this on the stove and heat the water to boiling; you may find it quicker to heat the water first in an electric kettle. This then forms a waterbath whereby the milk is heated indirectly. This way you have more control over the heating of the milk, and also it will be heated evenly, not hot at the bottom whilst the top is still cold.

Keep the water simmering until the temperature of the milk is 71°C (160°F), stirring occasionally. Hold this temperature for 15 seconds. This is the pasteurization temperature, which will kill all the disease-causing organisms.

Then cool the milk at once by covering and putting the container into cold water. Ideally the water should be running to continuously take the heat away, so change the water frequently until the right temperature of 4.5°C (40°F), is reached. Place in the refrigerator or another suitable cold place so that the milk remains at this temperature until used. You may find it quicker and easier to pasteurize small quantities at a time.

Curds and whey and fresh milk cheese

Curds and whey were probably the first products made by man from milk and were used extensively in cookery in medieval times. Curds form the basis of a number of recipes in this book and are extremely easy to make.

500ml (1 pt) milk makes 100–125g (4–5 oz) curds
500ml (1 pt) milk plus 50g (2 oz) dried skimmed milk powder makes
  150–200g (6–8 oz) curds

Use pasteurized milk only, as the rennet will not act with sterilized, ultra-heat-treated or boiled milk (see p. 13). Skimmed milk can be used.

Heat the milk in a double saucepan or bowl standing in a saucepan of simmering water until it reaches 38°C (100°F). If you have just pasteurized your milk, cool it to this temperature. If milk is limited and you wish to increase the quantity of curds obtained from a small amount of milk, you can add some milk powder. Stir in about 50g (2 oz) per 500ml (1 pt) milk at this stage. Dissolve the rennet tablet (1 tablet to 500ml (1 pt) milk) in a little warm water, add to the warm milk and stir in well. If rennet essence is used stir in 1 teaspoon per 500ml (1 pt) milk. Cover the container and leave in a warm place for 1 hour until set.

Line a sieve or colander with a square of butter muslin of double thickness. Stand this in a bowl. Then ladle thin slices of curd into the muslin. As you slice into the curd, watery liquid appears: this is the whey. Gather the corners of the cloth together and tie a piece of string tightly round to make a bag. Hang on a hook with a bowl underneath to catch the whey. Leave to drain for 2–3 hours.

Store the curds and whey in separate containers in the refrigerator for up to 2–3 days. The curds have a bland taste and smooth texture and the taste can be improved by the addition of a little salt. For recipes using curds in this book see Index.

Traditionally curds and whey are often served together, the curd swimming in a dish of whey. Fresh cream is poured over and sugar sprinkled on top. To give the curd a pleasing shape for this dish, you can use a mould in the draining stage.

Small moulds can be made from old margarine tubs, yoghurt or cream cartons. Cut out the bottoms so that they form hollow cylinders. Place upright in the muslin-lined container. If several moulds are to be filled, a stainless-steel cake rack can be placed in a large roasting tin to collect the whey. Several thicknesses of muslin should be laid on top of the cake rack and the moulds stood on this.

Ladle thin slices of curd into the mould as evenly as possible. If the curd slices overflow in the mould, wait a while to allow the curd to drain and sink a little, then fill with remaining curd. The curd will eventually sink to about halfway in the mould. Leave to drain for several hours, then carefully turn the mould over and leave to drain a little longer so that there is an even surface on both sides. Store as before.

Fresh milk cheese is made from this simple curd, either moulded or drained in the bag. Sprinkle salt over the surface of the moulded curd; it will be absorbed inwards. 'Spermyse' (herb cheese) can be made by rolling the curd in chopped fresh or dried herbs; their flavours too will be absorbed inwards.

The curd can also be beaten or sieved to make it smooth and then mixed with a variety of herbs and spices, chopped onion or garlic and salt. Add a little yoghurt or lemon juice for a sharper flavour. Pat the cheese into shape. Store in the refrigerator for 2–3 days.

Making other soft cheeses

Most hard and soft cheeses do require a cheese 'starter', a carefully grown culture of lactic bacteria which is used to sour the pasteurized milk and contributes to the finished flavour of the cheese. Cheese starter can be obtained by post from various dairy companies or agricultural colleges, and recently a sachet of freeze-dried culture has become available in some health food shops; but it does need careful maintenance and recultivation. This is not difficult once you have mastered the technique and can be done easily at home. However to go into detail here would be beyond the scope of this book. Those who wish to learn about these processes and make their own cheeses at home are advised to read my book, *Making Cheeses,* where full details of the equipment and ingredients needed, sterilization techniques and methods for making a variety of cheeses from the traditional soft Crowdie and Cambridge to the hard and larger Smallholder and Small Cheshire are given.

There is one lactic culture which is readily and cheaply available however and this is the culture in yoghurt. There are many different types of lactic bacteria, each requiring different conditions for growth, each giving a characteristic taste to a particular product. The cheese starter culture is the best one for cheese, but a yoghurt culture can be used for making a soft cheese as well as a soured cream and a cultured buttermilk albeit with a slight 'yoghurt' flavour. Provided a new fresh yoghurt is used for each batch of dairy products and care is taken with ingredients and equipment, successful results can be obtained.

Acid curd cheeses

These are the cheeses which are made by the action of acid on the milk protein, and include the traditional sour milk or lactic cheese. In the past this cheese was often made from raw milk which had soured and it is true that many families thrived on it without coming to much harm. The acidity does prevent the growth of harmful organisms to a certain extent, but you can never be entirely sure that it is completely free. If you do have a supply of raw milk which has soured normally and clotted and smells cleanly acid, you can make lactic cheese but use this cheese only in cooked dishes, and then you will be sure that the cooking temperatures kill any disease organisms which may be present. The curd is put in a muslin bag to drain, the time depending on the amount of curd initially; it can be scraped from the sides of the cloth occasionally to help drainage.

Never use pasteurized milk which has 'gone off'; pasteurized milk does not sour normally. It keeps for longer initially because the heat treatment destroys nearly all the lactic acid bacteria. If it does 'go off' when it is fairly old it may have been contaminated by other bacteria which could be harmful. It is always best to throw such milk away. To make lactic cheese from pasteurized milk you must use a cheese starter and this is described fully in my book *Making Cheeses.*

Lemon cheese

This is an acid curd cheese, but the acidity in this case is provided by the lemon juice.

500ml (1 pt) milk makes 100–125g (4–5 oz) cheese

Heat 500ml of milk to 38°C (100°F) in a double saucepan or bowl standing in a saucepan of simmering water. Remove the bowl from the hot water; add the juice of 1 lemon to the milk and stir well. Leave for 15 minutes. You will notice that the milk immediately separates into rather stringy curds and whey. Line a sieve or colander with muslin and stand this in a bowl. Pour the curd and whey into the muslin, gather the corners of the cloth together and tie with a piece of string. Hang over a bowl and leave for 1 hour to drain. Remove the cheese from the muslin; you may have to scrape it off the sides with a knife. Add a little salt to taste. The cheese is now ready to eat. It has a moist, spreadable texture and a very pleasant, slightly lemon taste. The lemon whey should be saved as it can be used in many recipes, and if well chilled, makes a refreshing drink.

Yoghurt cheese

You can use bought or home-made yoghurt for this cheese.

500ml (1 pt) thin yoghurt makes 100–150g (4–6 oz) cheese
500ml (1 pt) thick yoghurt makes 150–200g (6–8 oz) cheese

Heat the yoghurt in a double saucepan to 38°C (100°F) and then pour into the sieve or colander lined with muslin. Hang up the muslin bag and leave to drain for several hours. It may be necessary to scrape the cheese from the sides of the muslin and mix with the soft cheese in the centre to help drainage. The amount of cheese you obtain, its texture and moisture content depends on the draining time. A shorter draining time will give a larger amount of moister cheese. Experiment to suit your personal taste. Remove from the muslin and add salt to taste. You can also mix in chopped fresh or dried herbs, spices or chopped onions. Pat into shape. Store in the refrigerator for 4–5 days. This acid curd cheese can be used in many recipes.

Making yoghurt

Each country has its own soured or cultured milk, each one with a slightly different taste and texture according to the type of milk used and the culture present. Yoghurt is the traditional cultured milk of the Balkans, Greece, Turkey and Bulgaria, and comes to us from there. It has become very popular in recent years, especially the sweetened fruit variety, as it is an easy and convenient dessert. Yoghurt does not have the unique properties claimed which ensure long and healthy life, but it is a good food nevertheless because it is made from milk, and is easily digested, so can be given to old and young alike.

Yoghurt can be made at home, either in the special yoghurt-making machines, but these are relatively expensive, or in improvised equipment. Raw, pasteurized, sterilized, ultra-heat-treated, whole or skimmed milks can be used. Boil raw or pasteurized milk for 1 minute first, then cool to 43°C (110°F) by placing the pan in a bowl of cold water. This boiling is needed to destroy the micro-organisms in the milk and thus ensure that the yoghurt culture grows well; it makes the milk a better medium than just pasteurization. Sterilized or ultra-heat-treated milks do not need boiling as their initial heat treatment is sufficient, just heat to 43°C (110°F).

You are now ready to add your yoghurt culture to the milk. It is important that this yoghurt is as fresh as possible, to ensure that the culture is active and will work well. Its activity diminishes as it becomes older. Also it is advisable to use a new yoghurt each time you make your own yoghurt as contamination could occur if a portion of the home-made yoghurt is saved to act as a culture for the next batch. It is still economical as you can use this small carton to make a large amount of yoghurt and yoghurt cheese, to make sour cream and buttermilk. If you wish to make successive batches from one yoghurt culture it is wiser to obtain a laboratory-grown culture from a dairy company or agricultural college and maintain and recultivate it in the same way as a cheese starter. I described this in *Making Cheeses.*

Add 1–2 tbsp yoghurt to each 500ml (1 pt) milk; mix with a little of the prepared milk to make a smooth paste first, then gradually add the rest of the milk and stir well to ensure good distribution of the culture throughout the milk. Pour the milk into a suitable container or containers; you can use old yoghurt cartons for individual yoghurts. Cover and leave in a warm place for 3–6 hours to allow the culture to grow and clot the milk. Yoghurt culture needs a temperature of about 43°C (110°F) at which to grow. Your linen cupboard may be as hot as this, or a place near a solid fuel stove, so check with a room thermometer. If you do not have a suitable place as hot as this, cover your container with insulating material such as a small blanket, towel or nappy to keep the heat inside and then put in the warmest place possible. Alternatively you can use a wide-necked vacuum flask; this will maintain the temperature of the milk. It will need careful cleaning and sterilization afterwards.

When the yoghurt has set, it should be placed in the refrigerator; this will slow down the growth of the culture. However, growth does continue slowly even in cold conditions so that you find that the yoghurt gradually becomes more acid.The yoghurt made in a vacuum flask should be poured into another container; it can be stirred well to make it smooth and then placed in the refrigerator. This method gives a fairly thin yoghurt with a mild acid flavour. If you like a yoghurt with a sharper flavour, incubate for slightly longer until it suits your taste.

For a thick yoghurt similar to commercial shop-bought yoghurts either boil the milk initially for a longer time so that the volume is reduced by a quarter or a half and it becomes more concentrated, or add 50g (2 oz) dried skimmed milk powder per 500ml (1 pt) milk, after boiling. The commercial yoghurt is usually a thick yoghurt as dried milk is added in its manufacture.

Make fruit yoghurt by stirring in fruit or jam after it has set and chilled. Sweeten to taste by adding sugar or honey.

Producing cream at home

If you have a supply of raw milk available you may wish to separate your own cream. Pour the warm milk, fresh from the cow, into a large shallow pan or bowl, cover and leave to stand for 24 hours in a cool place or in the refrigerator so that the fat comes to the surface and forms a thin layer of cream. If you are using goat's milk you will have to leave it longer to allow the smaller fat globules to rise. Do not leave any strong-smelling substance near the milk since the cream easily absorbs flavours.

Now skim the cream off carefully using your skimmer or a thin-edged saucer. If you use the special perforated skimmer, the skimmed milk drains back into the pan. Start by breaking off at the pan edges; it will peel back like a thick skin. At first the consistency of the cream will vary a great deal, and some of the fat will be left in the skimmed milk. But with practice you will become more skilled. The cream should have a butterfat content of about 50 per cent, similar to double cream. If you want a thinner cream similar to single cream you can dilute your cream with an equal quantity of skimmed milk. Single cream is a pouring cream; it will not whip as the butterfat content is too low. A special whipping cream is available from grocery shops and dairies; this has a minimum of 35 per cent fat and should whip up to twice its volume. Again you can make your own whipping cream by diluting with a quarter of the quantity of skimmed milk, for example 125ml (¼ pt) skimmed milk to 500ml (1 pt) double cream.

It is possible to separate the cream from bottled, bought milk. Many people use 'top of the milk' as a pouring cream, but if you are careful you can obtain a 'whipping' cream. Leave the milk in the refrigerator for a day until the cream layer is quite distinct, then pour off the top 2 tablespoons very carefully. This will whip up lightly and can be used in recipes where a whipping cream is required, or for making small quantities of butter and buttermilk. Nine to ten tablespoons will give you about 125–150ml (¼ pt); this can be collected from 5 bottles of milk over 2 days.

The skimmed milk can be used as ordinary milk; for making cheese and yoghurt, and in cooking, or drunk by the diet conscious member of the family.

Pasteurization of home-produced cream

Again, it is advisable to pasteurize your cream. You may wonder why you do not pasteurize the milk first and then separate the cream to save doing it twice for cream and the skimmed milk. However, if you do this you will not have so much cream since pasteurization affects the structure of the fat globule slightly and the subsequent cream rise. Pour the cream into a bucket or bowl and place this in a larger container filled with boiling water as for milk pasteurization (see p. 15). Raise the temperature of the cream to 80°C (175°F), stirring occasionally and hold for 15 seconds. Cool at once to 4.5°C (40°F) by putting the container of cream into cold water.

Whipping cream

Whipping or double cream can be used for whipping; it should be aged and cooled first. This means keeping it at 4.5°C (40°F) for at least 24 hours; during pasteurization the fat melts partially and cooling allows it to resolidify. This applies to bought cream as well, as it may have become warm during transport to your home. After aging you will notice that the cream is thicker. The equipment for whipping, the whisk and the bowl, should be cold too; they can be left in the refrigerator for a time or cooled under water. Use a hand balloon whisk for the best results. Whip the cream quickly at first until it has a matt finish, and then slowly until it stands in peaks. Be careful not to overwhip or you will have butter before you know it. This also happens if the cream is too warm; butter forms even before the cream begins to increase in volume.

Clotted cream

Clotted cream can be made from double cream, the simplest method being to scald the cream in a double saucepan. Heat the cream to 77°–88°C (170°–190°F) and keep it at this temperature until the surface becomes thick and crusty, with a wrinkled appearance. This may take from ½–1 hour depending on the amount of cream you are clotting. Stir it occasionally at first to ensure even heating. As the cream is being scalded you do not need to pasteurize first. When ready remove the top saucepan or bowl and cool rapidly by placing in cold water. Leave in the refrigerator for 24 hours. It can than be packed in small glass jars or plastic containers. Store in the refrigerator for 4–5 days.

Soured cream

Yoghurt can be used to sour cream, which then has a pleasant piquant flavour. Use the same method as described for making yoghurt from milk (see p. 18). Boil single cream and add 1–2 tbsp fresh yoghurt to each 500ml (1 pt) cream. Pour into suitable containers and incubate at 43°C (110°F) for about 6 hours. If you want a mildly acid cream do not incubate for so long. You can also sour cream by adding lemon juice; add 2 tbsp to 125ml (¼ pt) cream.

Cream cheese

Cream cheese is usually made with a cheese starter to give a pleasant, slightly acid flavour to the cheese and to improve its keeping quality. A very acceptable cream cheese can be made with the soured cream produced (see p. 21). Leave to incubate for 6 hours until set. Mix in a little salt (about 1 tsp per 500ml (1 pt) cream) and pour into a muslin-lined sieve or colander. Hang up the muslin bag and leave to drain for about 8 hours. Scrape the cheese from the sides of the cloth and mix with the softer cheese in the centre occasionally to help the cheese drain. The cloth can also be changed at intervals. Pat into shape and keep in plastic containers in the refrigerator for 4–5 days.

Making butter

Use double or whipping cream for making butter. Those who have their own supply of cream will certainly wish to make butter; it is not economical to make it from bought double or whipping cream, but you can use the 'whipping' cream separated from the top of the milk for making small quantities of butter.

500ml (1 pt) of cream will make about 150–200g (6–8 oz) butter

First separate your cream, pasteurize it and keep it cool until you have collected sufficient to make the amount of butter you require (but none of it should be more than 3 days old).

The churning temperature of the butter is important; it should be between 10°–16°C (50°–60°F) depending on the season, lower in hot summer weather and higher in cooler weather. Pour the cream into the bowl or churn jar you are using for the churning and stand in warm or cold water to bring it to the right temperature. A jam jar can be used very effectively for churning small quantities of cream (as I discovered when making our daily butter supplies whilst living in Africa). Do not fill the container more than half full. Stand the wooden board and scotch hands or wooden spoons in clean cold water until used.

Now beat or churn your cream. If you use an electric beater set it at slow speed. Just shake the jam jar up and down to simulate the churning action. Gradually the cream will thicken and then begin to separate into butter grains and buttermilk. If necessary add some cold water (at about 10°C, 50°F) and churn again. This is known as breaking water and helps to separate and round off the grains. The yellow butter will begin to stick together in a solid lump. Pour off the buttermilk and save this. Pour cold water over the butter grains to wash them, churn for a few seconds, and then run off the water. Repeat the washings until the water runs off as a clear liquid; this is important so that all buttermilk is removed. If some remains the butter will not keep and may go rancid.

Tip the butter into a muslin cloth, press out the water, and if the butter
has become soft leave it in a cool place to harden a little. Next the butter
must be worked to remove as much water as possible, so that it will keep.
You do this by putting it on the wooden or formica board and pressing
with the scotch hands or wooden spoon; press it down into a thin layer,
fold over and press down again. The water will appear as small droplets,
and if you slope the board slightly these can run off. If the butter becomes
soft again while working, harden in a cool place for a while. Salt can be
added at the same time, 1–2 tsp per 500g (1 lb) butter. Finally pat the
butter into shape – round, rectangular, cylindrical or what you will, and
wrap in greaseproof paper or tin foil.

Buttermilk

Buttermilk has a good food value as it contains most of the other milk
constituents. Use as a drink and for cooking. You can make your own
cultured buttermilk with a yoghurt culture. Boil the buttermilk first and
follow the directions for making yoghurt (see p. 18). You can make it thin
and suitable for drinking, or thick for cooking purposes, and alter the
acidity according to your taste with a shorter or longer incubating time.

Clarified butter

Butter, although it is essentially a fat, contains water and a small
proportion of other milk constituents. It can be cleared of these by the
process of clarification, and is then a much better medium for frying as it
will not spit or burn so easily – and it gives a better flavour to the food. In
the Middle Ages butter was always reduced in this way for cooking
purposes. Clarified butter also provides an effective airtight seal for pâté,
terrines and potted meats.

To clarify butter melt the butter gently over a low heat in a heavy
saucepan. Let it bubble for a few minutes, then remove from the heat.
Leave to stand for several minutes and pour through a double thickness of
butter muslin into a jar if not needed immediately. The strained, melted
butter will be clear and free of milk solids. Keep in the refrigerator. It will
resolidify.

3 Soups

The earliest soups were the thick cereal-based pottages made by man ever since he began to boil his food in a cooking pot. To the basic brew were added seeds, leaves, roots of wild plants, fruits, nuts and pulses. Right through the Middle Ages pottage was still enjoyed by all classes of people: the oatmeal porridge of the north, the rice pottage of the rich made with almonds and spices as an accompaniment to meat, the barley frumenty of the poor and the pease pottage served with bacon for the gentry, and without for the peasant's family. But by the end of the seventeenth century and during the eighteenth century a thin pottage began to be served on its own as a first course and was known as 'soupe'.

'Soupe' was based on meat, or fish stock rather than cereals. Vegetable soups were made from herbs, legumes or roots boiled in water. The famous turtle and eel soups, pea and game soups came into fashion.

Now soup can be an appetizer or a meal in itself; all can be nourishing if made with milk. Simple vegetable soups can be made from puréed vegetables and milk. Just fry the chopped vegetables in a little butter first, then simmer in water or stock until soft. Sieve or liquidize to a purée and reheat, adding the milk. And many soups are enhanced by the addition of several spoons of cream, fresh or soured, just before serving.

Pease Soup *Serves 4*

This eighteenth century soup has all the flavour of a summer herb and vegetable garden.

250g (8 oz) fresh or frozen peas
1 stick of celery, sliced
1 small onion, sliced
2–3 sprigs of mint, chopped
15g (½ oz) butter
salt and pepper

¼ tsp ground cloves
½ tsp nutmeg
1 tbsp chopped parsley
300ml (½ pt) milk or single cream
To serve: croûtons, lemon slices

Cook the peas in slightly salted water until tender. Drain, keeping 300ml (½ pt) of the cooking liquid. Fry the celery, onion and mint gently in butter. Add to peas and cooking liquid and liquidize or sieve to a purée. Add salt and pepper, ground cloves, nutmeg, chopped parsley and reheat. When almost boiling add the milk or cream. Serve with fried croûtons (see Appendix 1) and slices of lemon.

Cheese Pottage *Serves 4*

This is an eighteenth century English version of French onion soup.

350g (12 oz) onions
25g (1 oz) butter
900ml (1½ pt) beef stock
salt and pepper

4 hard boiled eggs, finely chopped
150g (6 oz) grated Cheddar or Cheshire cheese
4 slices of French bread, about 2½cm (1 in)
    thick

Slice the onions and fry gently in butter until tender but not brown. Pour in stock, salt and pepper and bring to the boil. Simmer for 30 minutes. Add the hard boiled eggs and 50g (2 oz) of the grated cheese. Stir until cheese has melted. Pour into 4 individual heatproof soup dishes or one large soup tureen. Place bread floating on top of the soup and sprinkle the remaining cheese on top of each slice. Brown under hot grill and serve immediately.

Almond Soup *Serves 4*

This soup goes back to medieval times when almonds were used extensively in cookery. Often they were pounded with rosewater to make almond milk, a substitute for cow's milk on fasting days.

600ml (1 pt) chicken stock
300ml (½ pt) milk
1 bayleaf
50g (2 oz) ground almonds
½ tsp almond essence
1 egg yolk or ½ tbsp cornflour

4 tbsp single cream
½ tsp nutmeg
salt and pepper
1–2 tbsp lemon juice or soured cream
  (optional)
To serve: 25g (1 oz) roasted almonds

Simmer the chicken stock, milk and bayleaf with the ground almonds and essence for 20 minutes. Remove the bayleaf and liquidize or sieve the soup. Mix the egg yolk or cornflour with the cream and gradually add to the hot liquid. Reheat gently to thicken but do not boil. Add nutmeg and salt and pepper to taste, and stir in lemon juice or soured cream if used. Serve with roasted almonds.

Bean Soup *Serves 4*

Here is the traditional bean pottage made into a rich soup together with the accompanying flavour of bacon. In the past beans were an important part of the English diet, and it is a pity that we do not eat more pulses now, because they are so nourishing.

175g (6 oz) dried haricot beans
900ml (1½ pt) water or stock
25g (1 oz) butter or bacon fat
4 rashers streaky bacon, chopped
1 onion, chopped
1 carrot, chopped

1 sprig each of parsley, thyme and
  marjoram
300ml (½ pt) milk
salt and pepper
To serve: 1 tbsp chopped parsley

Soak the beans in water overnight. Melt the fat and fry the bacon, onion and carrot gently for 10 minutes. Add the beans, the water or stock and herbs, bring to the boil and simmer for 2 hours or until the beans are soft. A pressure cooker can be used to reduce the cooking time if liked; if so, cook at 15 lb pressure for 30 minutes and use 600ml (1 pt) water or stock.

Remove the herbs and sieve or liquidize to make a purée. Measure the quantity: you should have about 900ml (1½ pt) purée, if not, make up with water. Reheat, add the milk and season to taste with salt and pepper. Serve sprinkled with chopped parsley.

Cream of Mushroom Soup *Serves 4*

250g (8 oz) mushrooms   600ml (1 pt) milk
2 onions   salt and pepper
50g (2 oz) butter   150ml (¼ pt) single cream
25g (1 oz) flour

Chop the mushrooms and onions and fry gently in 25g (1 oz) butter. Sieve or liquidize to a purée. Melt the rest of the butter in a saucepan, add the flour and cook for a few minutes. Remove from the heat, add the milk gradually, return to the heat and simmer for five minutes. Add the mushroom purée and seasoning to taste. Remove from the heat, blend in the cream and serve immediately.

Nettle or Spinach Soup *Serves 4*

Richard Mabey in *Food for Free* says that nettles should not be picked for eating after the beginning of June as the leaves become coarse, bitter tasting and decidedly laxative. The best time of all for them is when the shoots are no more than a few inches high. If you are gathering later in the year, pick just the tops and the young, pale green leaves. Remove the tougher stems and wash well.

250g (8 oz) nettles or spinach leaves   1 tsp sugar
25g (1 oz) butter   600ml (1 pt) chicken stock
1 onion, sliced   300ml (½ pt) milk
1 carrot, sliced   1–2 tbsp lemon juice
1 stick of celery, sliced   *To serve:* cheese tartlets, single
salt and pepper   cream

Boil the nettle or spinach leaves for a few minutes in 1–2 tbsp water. Fry onion, carrot and celery gently in butter in a saucepan. Add nettles or spinach, seasoning, sugar and chicken stock. Bring to the boil and simmer for 20 minutes. Sieve or liquidize to a purée. Reheat, add the milk and lemon juice. Serve with little cheese tartlets (see p. 60). A spoon of cream swirled into each plate adds an attractive contrast to the green colour of the soup.

Chilled Potato and Leek Soup (Vichyssoise) *Serves 4*

250g (8 oz) leeks, chopped
1 small onion, chopped
25g (1 oz) butter
250g (8 oz) potatoes, peeled and sliced
600ml (1 pt) chicken stock

salt and pepper
pinch of nutmeg
300ml (½ pt) single or double
  cream
To serve: 2 tbsp chopped chives

Fry the leeks and onion gently in butter in a saucepan until soft, but do not allow to brown. Add the potatoes with the stock, salt, pepper and nutmeg. Bring to the boil, then simmer for 30 minutes or until the potatoes are soft. Sieve or liquidize, and chill. Just before serving stir in the cream and sprinkle with chopped chives.

If liked, this soup can be served hot; if so, reheat the vegetable purée and then stir in the cream.

Yoghurt and Mint Soup *Serves 4*

An adaptation of a Middle Eastern recipe.

600ml (1 pt) chicken stock
50g (2 oz) noodles
300ml (½ pt) thick yoghurt

1 egg
salt and pepper
2 tbsp chopped fresh mint

Bring the stock to the boil and cook noodles until tender. Beat yoghurt and egg together and heat gently, stirring constantly until the mixture thickens. Stir in the stock and noodles. Season to taste and serve. Sprinkle with the mint.

4 Sauces

English food is nowadays often thought to be plain and unappetizing and this may be because it is served without a sauce, except perhaps the inevitable bottle of tomato ketchup. Most dishes are enhanced by the accompaniment of a suitable sauce since the palate requires food to be moist rather than dry to appreciate its full flavour; the Englishman of the past always enjoyed his sauces. There were the piquant rich medieval sauces made from breadcrumbs and herbs, the sweet and sour sauces of vinegar, sugar and spices, and the citrus fruit and wine sauces of Elizabethan times. Each dish had its own special sauce.

Gradually the types of sauces changed and the ones enjoyed in the eighteenth century have become our traditional sauces. Although not as highly spiced as their medieval precursors, there is a rich range, a number of delicious sauces from which to choose for each dish and most are very simple to make.

Milk and cream form the liquid base of many of our sauces. I include a selection but not by any means all. The modern ingredients, yoghurt and soft cheese, can also be used as a base, especially for a piquant sauce.

Sauces can be served separately as an accompaniment, or with the meat, fish or vegetables as an integral part of the dish.

Hot sauces

Bread Sauce *Serves 4–6*

Bread sauce is one of our oldest sauces. In medieval times almonds and breadcrumbs were used as thickening agents rather than flour; fine ground flour was a luxury and it was only later that it came to be used for thickening. This can be seen in the many traditional recipes for puddings, rissoles, meat loaves, possets and tansies which incorporate breadcrumbs.

1 small onion	25g (1 oz) butter
3 or 4 cloves	salt and pepper
300ml (½ pt) milk	½ tsp nutmeg
50g (2 oz) fresh white breadcrumbs	2 tbsp single cream (optional)

Peel the onion and stick cloves into it. Put into a saucepan with the milk and simmer gently for 20 minutes to allow the flavours to infuse the milk. Remove the onion and add the breadcrumbs. Stir in the butter, salt and pepper and the nutmeg and heat very gently so that the breadcrumbs swell, but keep below simmering point. Stir in the cream and serve hot with roast chicken or turkey.

White Sauce

The flour and butter roux was introduced late in the seventeenth century and gradually replaced breadcrumbs as a thickener for sauces and soups.

The common white sauce is the basis of many other sauces and can be made thin as a pouring sauce or thick to coat.

Here are the basic recipes:

Pouring Sauce Serves 4–6

15g (½ oz) butter   300ml (½ pt) milk
15g (½ oz) flour   salt and pepper

Melt the butter, add the flour and cook over a low heat for 2 minutes without allowing the mixture (the roux) to brown. Remove from the heat and gradually add the milk, mixing in well. Heat, stirring all the time until the sauce comes to the boil and thickens. Simmer gently for 3 minutes. Season to taste with salt and pepper.

To make more or less sauce, alter all the ingredients accordingly, for example, to make 450ml (¾ pt) sauce use 20g (¾ oz) butter, 20g (¾ oz) flour and 450ml (¾ pt) milk.

Coating Sauce Serves 4

25g (1 oz) butter   300ml (½ pt) milk
25g (1 oz) flour   salt and pepper

Cook as for pouring sauce.

To make 150ml (¼ pt) sauce use 15g (½ oz) butter, 15g (½ oz) flour and 150ml (¼ pt) milk; use 50g (2 oz), 50g (2 oz) and 600ml (1 pt) for 600ml (1 pt) sauce.

White sauce can also be made with half white stock and half milk; for a richer sauce, single cream can be substituted for some of the milk. For a more piquant sauce stir in 1–2 tbsp yoghurt or soured cream just before adding the seasoning, but do not allow to reboil.

Anchovy Sauce

Add 1–2 tsp anchovy essence and 1 tsp lemon juice to 300ml (½ pt) white pouring or coating sauce made with half fish stock and half milk, or all milk. Serve with fish, and fried veal dishes.

Cheese Sauce

Stir in 50–75g (2–3 oz) grated Cheddar or crumbled Lancashire cheese, 1 tsp made mustard, a pinch of cayenne pepper and 1 tsp lemon juice to 300ml (½ pt) white pouring or coating sauce. Do not reboil the sauce. Serve with fish, poultry, bacon, egg and vegetable dishes.

Egg Sauce

Stir in 1 finely chopped hard boiled egg to 300ml (½ pt) white pouring or coating sauce. Serve with fish or chicken.

Lemon Sauce

Stir in finely grated rind of ½ lemon and 2 tbsp lemon juice to 300ml (½ pt) white pouring or coating sauce. Do not allow to boil after adding the lemon juice. Serve with fish, chicken, veal or egg dishes.

Mustard Sauce

Mix 2 tsp dry mustard with 2 tsp vinegar and then whisk into 300ml (½ pt) white pouring or coating sauce with 1 tsp sugar. Serve with herring, mackerel, cheese and ham.

Parsley Sauce

Stir in 1–2 tbsp finely chopped parsley to 300ml (½ pt) white pouring or coating sauce. Serve with bacon, ham and fish.

Rich White Sauce (Béchamel) *Serves 4*

The béchamel is of course a French sauce, but is found in the recipe books of the eighteenth century. It is just a richer white sauce, the milk being first infused with the flavours of various vegetables and herbs. Eliza Acton describes it as 'a fine French white sauce, now very much served at good English tables. It may be made in various ways, and more or less expensively, but it should always be thick, smooth and rich, though delicate in flavour'.

300ml (½ pt) milk	6 peppercorns
1 small onion, peeled and sliced	1 sprig of parsley
small piece of celery, sliced	25g (1 oz) butter
1 bayleaf	25g (1 oz) flour
2 cloves	salt and pepper
1 blade of mace	2 tbsp single or soured cream (optional)

Put the milk, vegetables, herbs and spices in a saucepan and bring slowly to the boil. Remove from the heat, cover and leave in a warm place to infuse for 30 minutes. Strain the milk. Now make a roux with the butter and flour as for the white sauce and add the flavoured milk gradually as before. Heat, stirring until the sauce comes to the boil and thickens. Simmer gently for 3 minutes. Season to taste and stir in the cream. Serve with chicken, veal, fish and vegetable dishes.

The béchamel is used as the basis for a number of other sauces:

Hot Horseradish Sauce

Stir in 1 tbsp grated horseradish, 1 tsp vinegar and ½ tsp sugar to 300ml (½ pt) béchamel sauce. Serve with roast beef and grilled steak, grilled trout, mackerel and herring.

Mock Hollandaise Sauce

Stir in 1–2 egg yolks mixed first with 2 tbsp single cream, and 2 tsp lemon juice or wine vinegar to 300ml (½ pt) béchamel sauce. Reheat without boiling. Serve with poached, steamed or grilled fish.

Mornay Sauce

Stir in one egg yolk mixed first with 2 tbsp single cream, and 50g (2 oz) grated Cheddar cheese to 300ml (½ pt) béchamel sauce. Reheat without boiling. Serve with fish or vegetables.

Tartare Sauce

Stir in 1 egg yolk mixed first with 2 tbsp single cream, 1 tbsp finely chopped parsley, 2 tsp finely chopped gherkins, 2 tsp chopped capers and 2 tsp lemon juice or wine vinegar to 300ml (½ pt) béchamel sauce. Reheat without boiling. Serve with fish dishes.

Onion Sauce *Serves 4–6*

2 onions
300ml (½ pt) milk
25g (1 oz) butter

25g (1 oz) flour
salt and pepper

Peel the onions and chop finely. Cook in milk for about 20 minutes until tender. Melt the butter, add flour and cook over a low heat for 2 minutes. Gradually add the milk and onions, stirring all the time. Season and simmer for a few minutes. Serve with lamb, mutton, rabbit or tripe.

Yoghurt Sauce *Serves 4*

1 whole egg or 2 egg yolks
150ml (¼ pt) thick yoghurt

salt and pepper
chopped fresh herbs

Beat the egg and stir in the yoghurt. Heat very gently, stirring in one direction all the time. At first the yoghurt will become thinner and then it will gradually thicken so that it coats the spoon thickly. Add salt and pepper to taste and chopped fresh herbs of your choice. Serve hot or cold with meat, chicken, or fish. As a cold sauce it makes a good salad dressing.

Cold sauces and salad dressings

English Salad Sauce *Serves 4*

This is one of Eliza Acton's recipes.

2 hard boiled eggs   pinch of cayenne   150ml (¼ pt) single cream
pinch of salt   pepper   1–2 tbsp vinegar
¼ tsp sugar   1 tsp water

Remove the yolks from the hard boiled eggs and mash to a paste with the back of a spoon. Mix in the salt, sugar, cayenne pepper and water. Then stir in the cream gradually. Add the vinegar. This is a light but rich salad dressing. Serve with mixed vegetable salads.

Sour Cream Sauce *Serves 4*

2 tbsp lemon juice
2 tbsp thin yoghurt   } or 300ml (½ pt) soured cream
150ml (¼ pt) single or double cream
½ tsp sugar   1 tbsp chopped fresh herbs, or
salt and pepper   chives (optional)

Mix together the lemon juice, yoghurt and cream; add the sugar and salt and pepper to taste, and the herbs or chives if required. Chill. Serve as a salad dressing, or with grilled or cold meat, chicken or fish.

Horseradish Sauce *Serves 4*

150ml (¼ pt) double cream or thick yoghurt   2 tsp sugar
2 tbsp grated horseradish root   salt and pepper
1 tbsp wine vinegar or lemon juice

Lightly whip the cream, or stir the yoghurt until smooth. Mix in the horseradish, vinegar or lemon juice, sugar, salt and pepper to taste. Chill. Serve with beef.

Mustard Cream Sauce *Serves 4*

150ml (¼ pt) double or whipping cream   salt and pepper
2 tbsp made mustard

Lightly whip the cream and mix in the mustard, salt and pepper to taste. Serve with herring, mackerel and grilled meat.

Cream Cheese Sauce *Serves 4*

2 tbsp lemon juice   salt and pepper
2 tbsp single cream   1 tbsp chopped fresh herbs
125g (4 oz) acid curd or cream cheese   (optional)

Beat the lemon juice and cream into the cheese so that it becomes a thick, creamy sauce. Add salt, pepper and herbs if used. Serve with grilled meat or fish, as a dressing for coleslaw salad, or as a savoury dip.

Yoghurt Salad Dressing *Serves 4*

150ml (¼ pt) thin yoghurt   salt and pepper
1 tbsp lemon juice   1 tsp sugar (optional)
1 tsp made mustard

Beat the yoghurt with the lemon juice and mustard. Add salt and pepper to taste and sugar if required.

Butter sauces

Savoury butters

From medieval times the poor ate butter and herbs as a spread for their bread, and in the seventeenth century when butter was popular amongst all classes there were directions for making 'sundry sorts of most dainty butter, having a lively taste of sage, cinnamon, nutmeg, mace, etc.', as well as parsley and thyme butters.These were made with the extracted oils of the herbs and spices. We do not need to use the oils, but herbs or spices should be as finely chopped or ground as possible. The butter should be creamed until it is soft so that the flavouring works in well. After making, the butter should be well chilled and put onto the hot food just before serving so that it is beginning to melt as it is eaten. It can be stored in the refrigerator for a few days.

Cinnamon Butter *Serves 4*

50g (2 oz) butter   1 tsp powdered cinnamon   ½ tsp lemon juice

Cream the butter and work in the cinnamon and lemon juice. Form into pats and chill. Serve with grilled fish, potatoes, chicken or on toast.

Devilled Butter *Serves 4*

50g (2 oz) butter   pinch of cayenne pepper
1 tsp made mustard   1 tsp lemon juice
½ tsp curry powder

Cream the butter until soft and beat in the rest of the ingredients. Form into pats and chill. Serve with potatoes or grilled meat.

Garlic Butter *Serves 4*

2 cloves of garlic   50g (2 oz) butter

Peel the garlic cloves and boil in water for 5 minutes. Drain and chop finely. Cream the butter until soft and beat in the garlic. Form into pats and chill. Serve with grilled steak.

Green Butter *Serves 4*

50g (2 oz) butter   2 sprigs of mint   2 sprigs of parsley
1 small spinach leaf   2 sage leaves

Cream the butter until soft. Scald the herbs by pouring boiling water over them. Leave for a few minutes, drain and dry in a clean cloth. Chop very finely, then beat into the butter until well worked into it. Form into small pats and chill. Serve with fish, grilled steak or potatoes.

Lemon Butter *Serves 4*

50g (2 oz) butter   1 tsp grated lemon rind   1 tsp lemon juice

Cream the butter until soft. Beat in the lemon rind and juice. Form into pats and chill. Serve with fish or chicken.

Melted Butter Sauce *Serves 4*

This rich sauce was one of the popular sauces of the eighteenth century with the gentry; the poor had to be content with a plain white sauce with flour and little or no butter. This was the age when butter was used in all cooking, not only in cakes and pastry, for frying and basting, for potting of fish and meat, but also for pouring over meat and vegetable dishes and as a sauce for boiled puddings.

2 tsp flour   4 tbsp water
pinch of salt   50g (2 oz) butter
4 tbsp milk   1 tbsp lemon juice or wine vinegar (optional)

Mix the flour with the salt, and then mix in the milk and cold water gradually to make a smooth paste. Heat, bring to the boil and simmer for 2 minutes, then add the butter cut into small pieces. Stir until the butter has melted and simmer a minute. Add lemon juice or vinegar to sharpen the flavour. Serve with fish, grilled meat or vegetables. Chopped fennel or parsley may be added to serve with fish or meat.

Sweet butters

Brandy Butter (Hard Sauce) *Serves 4–6*

100g (4 oz) butter   75g (3 oz) icing sugar   1 tbsp brandy
75g (3 oz) caster sugar   25g (1 oz) ground almonds

Cream the butter until soft. Gradually beat in the sugar until light in texture, mix in almonds and brandy. Roll into small balls and serve with Christmas Pudding or other baked or steamed puddings.

Rum Butter *Serves 4–6*

100g (4 oz) butter   1 glass rum
150g (6 oz) soft brown sugar

Cream the butter until soft and beat in the sugar, until light and fluffy, then add the rum gradually. Roll into small balls and chill. Serve with steamed or baked puddings.

Wine Sauce *Serves 4*

This is a traditional recipe.

50g (2 oz) melted butter   150ml (¼ pt) sherry or wine
25g (1 oz) icing sugar

Stir the sugar and sherry into the melted butter and heat to the point of boiling. Serve with baked or steamed puddings.

Sauces for cakes and desserts

Sweet White Sauce *Serves 4–6*

This is a traditional recipe.

25g (1 oz) butter   300ml (½ pt) milk
15g (½ oz) flour   25g (1 oz) sugar

Melt the butter, and stir in the flour. Gradually add the milk and sugar, bring to the boil and simmer for a few minutes. Vanilla essence, almond essence, orange or lemon rind can be added for flavouring. Serve with steamed and baked puddings and ice cream. Other variations are:

Chocolate Sauce

To the Sweet White Sauce add 50g (2 oz) plain chocolate or 2 tbsp cocoa plus 2 tbsp sugar melted in a little hot water, and 1 tsp vanilla essence.

Brandy Sauce

To the Sweet White Sauce add 2 tbsp brandy.

Butterscotch Sauce

Use 75g (3 oz) brown sugar to make the Sweet White Sauce, and add 1 tsp vanilla essence.

Caramel Sauce

Omit the sugar in the Sweet White Sauce. Caramelize 50g (2 oz) sugar with 2 tbsp water by boiling together in a pan until light brown. Stir into the hot sauce.

Rich Chocolate Sauce *Serves 4*

25g (1 oz) plain chocolate	1 tsp rum	½ tsp vanilla essence
150ml (¼ pt) milk, or milk and cream	1 tbsp sugar	1 egg, separated

Grate the chocolate into the milk and heat so that the chocolate melts. Add rum, sugar and vanilla essence. Stir into the beaten egg yolk. Pour back into a saucepan and whisk over a low heat until light, frothy and thick. This can be done in a double saucepan. Beat egg white stiffly and fold in. Serve at once, with steamed or baked puddings or ice cream. It can be also be eaten on its own, but double the quantities for 4. If liked, the chocolate can be omitted and other flavourings used.

Custard Pudding Sauce *Serves 4–6*

Eliza Acton gives this recipe.

rind from ½ lemon	1 tbsp sugar	1 tsp flour
piece of cinnamon	300ml (½ pt) milk	pinch of salt
vanilla pod or 1 tsp vanilla essence	2 egg yolks or 1 whole egg	1 tbsp cold milk

Add the lemon rind, cinnamon, vanilla and sugar to the milk and bring to the boil. Simmer gently for a few minutes. Beat the egg yolks and mix in flour, salt and 1 tbsp milk. Strain the hot milk over the eggs, and then pour back into the saucepan. Heat very gently, whisking or stirring rapidly until it thickens and looks creamy and frothy. This can be done in a double saucepan. For sherry sauce add 2 tbsp sherry to the sauce when it is cooked. The lemon rind, cinnamon and vanilla can be replaced by other flavourings such as coffee powder, orange rind or grated chocolate. Serve with steamed or baked puddings.

Fruit Yoghurt Sauce *Serves 4–6*

150ml (¼ pt) fruit purée	1 tbsp lemon juice
150ml (¼ pt) either yoghurt, cultured buttermilk or soured cream	sugar

Mix the fruit purée and yoghurt (or buttermilk or soured cream) together with the lemon juice. Sweeten to taste. Serve with baked puddings and ice cream.

5 Vegetables
and salads

Vegetables have always been important in the English diet and our forebears ate a variety of vegetables and herbs, wild and cultivated, cooked and raw, which makes our present day selection seem very limited. Medieval kitchen gardens had their cabbage and leek enclosures; onions, carrots and pulses for drying were also grown by the poor peasant and he supplemented his meagre diet with roots, leaves and fruits gathered wild.

In Elizabethan times fresh salads were served as appetizers before meals. These salads consisted of a varied selection of vegetables, herbs and flowers dressed in vinegar and oil. The variety of different plants considered necessary for a well stocked kitchen garden was large, although these plants were also used for brewing medicinal potions, for flavouring and distilling.

The seventeenth century saw the development of market gardens especially around London and in the southeast, and new varieties such as cauliflowers and brussels sprouts were introduced from France and Flanders where market gardening had been important for some time. The potato (both sweet and Virginian), had of course been introduced in Elizabeth's reign from the Americas and was at first baked in sweet pies with dried fruits and spices, rather like the pumpkin pies which went to America and became a national dish there. Later potatoes were cooked as an accompaniment to savoury foods. The Irish rapidly took to growing potatoes as an easier crop than oats or barley, and they became their staple food. Similarly they were widely grown in the north of England. Potatoes were often eaten with milk or buttermilk and as such did not provide a bad diet, but rather monotonous. I include a number of the traditional milk and potato dishes.

Eighteenth and nineteenth century cooks understood well the art of cooking vegetables so that they retained much of their taste, texture and value and they served them in rich and varied sauces often with butter, cream or milk so that they were a veritable dish on their own and not a limp, tasteless and valueless accompaniment to the meat course. Now vegetables are regaining their prestige as many people grow their own in kitchen gardens and allotments. Modern technology ensures that we have a rich variety of high quality vegetables throughout the year be they frozen, imported or grown under special conditions. Many people too are inclined to the vegetarian way of life as healthier or economically necessary, and a wide range of vegetables cooked or uncooked and served with milk, cheese and eggs provide an interesting and nutritious diet.

Vegetables

Green Peas with Cream *Serves 4*

This recipe is taken from Hannah Glasse.

15g (½ oz) flour	pinch of nutmeg
25g (1 oz) butter, softened	1 tsp sugar
500g (1 lb) fresh or frozen peas	1 tbsp chopped parsley
salt and pepper	150ml (¼ pt) single or double cream

Mix the flour with the softened butter. Cook the peas in 150ml (¼ pt) boiling water and when tender add the flour and butter, salt and pepper to taste, nutmeg, sugar and chopped parsley. Heat, stirring all the time until the sauce comes to the boil and thickens. Stir in the cream and serve immediately.

Celery with Cream *Serves 4*

This is an eighteenth century recipe.

2 large heads of celery	salt and pepper
1–2 egg yolks	pinch of nutmeg
150ml (¼ pt) single or double cream	

Trim off the green tops of the celery, keeping a few pale green ones. Wash the stalks well and cut into pieces about 7cm (3 in) long. Boil in a little salted water until soft. Drain well. Beat the egg yolks with the cream, salt, pepper and nutmeg. Pour over the celery and heat gently, stirring all the time until it begins to thicken. Do not allow to boil. Serve immediately, garnished with some of the pale green leaves.

Spinach and Eggs *Serves 4*

This makes a good lunch or supper dish.

750g (1½ lb) spinach leaves	pinch of nutmeg
150ml (¼ pt) cream	4 slices of white bread
25g (1 oz) butter	butter for frying
salt and pepper	4 eggs

Wash the spinach well. Cook in a few tablespoons of water until tender. Drain. Sieve or liquidize to a purée, add the cream, butter, salt, pepper and nutmeg and heat gently until hot. Cut the bread into triangles and fry in butter as for croûtons (see Appendix 1). Keep warm. Poach the eggs. Pour the spinach into a shallow, buttered heatproof dish, arrange the eggs around the dish with the croûtons. Serve immediately.

Mushroom Fricassée on Toast *Serves 2–3*

250g (8 oz) mushrooms   150ml (¼ pt) single cream
50g (2 oz) butter   1 tsp nutmeg
rind of ½ lemon   salt and pepper
blade of mace   1 tbsp lemon juice
1 egg yolk   hot buttered toast

Wash and dry the mushrooms. Simmer gently in butter with lemon rind and mace for 10 minutes. Beat the egg yolk with the cream and nutmeg. Remove the mace from the mushrooms and add the cream. Stir until it thickens, then season to taste and add the lemon juice. Serve on top of hot buttered toast.

Sprouts with Cheese *Serves 4*

Cauliflower cheese is well known, but the cheese sauce goes well with a number of vegetables. The nutty flavour of sprouts blends particularly well.

500g (1 lb) sprouts   300ml (½ pt) cheese coating sauce
15g (½ oz) butter   (see p. 31)

Prepare the sprouts and boil in salted water until tender. Drain and shake well in the butter over the heat for 2 minutes. Pour the hot cheese sauce over the sprouts and serve.

Sour Baked Cabbage *Serves 4*

500g (1 lb) cabbage   salt and pepper
300ml (½ pt) soured cream or   2 tbsp breadcrumbs
  thick yoghurt   25g (1 oz) butter

Wash, quarter and shred the cabbage. Cook for a few minutes in boiling, salted water so that the cabbage retains its crispness. Drain and put in a buttered heatproof dish. Mix the soured cream or yoghurt with salt and pepper to taste, and pour over the cabbage. Cover with breadcrumbs and dot with butter. Bake for 20 minutes at 180°C (350°F), Mark 4.

Casseroled Potatoes *Serves 4*

750g (1½ lb) potatoes   salt and pepper
300ml (½ pt) milk   25g (1 oz) butter

Peel and thinly slice the potatoes. Dry well and arrange in layers in a buttered heatproof dish, seasoning between the layers. Pour in the milk and dot with butter. Bake at 190°C (375°F), Mark 5 for 1 hour.

Grated cheese and thinly sliced onions can also be put between the layers.

Stelk *Serves 4*

A traditional supper dish given by Dorothy Hartley in *Food in England*.

250g (8 oz) spring onions   50g (2 oz) butter
300ml (½ pt) milk   salt and pepper
500g (1 lb) potatoes

Trim and cut the onions into 1cm (½ in) lengths right up to the green tops. Simmer in milk until tender and strain, keeping the milk. Boil the potatoes until tender and then mash with the onion-flavoured milk. Beat until light. Add the onion pieces, 25g (1 oz) of the butter, salt and pepper. Make a well in the top of each serving and put a lump of butter to melt in it.

Pan Haggerty *Serves 4*

This is a traditional Northumberland recipe.

500g (1 lb) potatoes   125g (4 oz) grated Cheddar
250g (8 oz) onions   cheese
beef dripping   salt and pepper

Peel the potatoes and slice them very thinly, dry well. Peel and slice the onions thinly. Melt the dripping in a frying pan, remove from the heat and put in alternate layers of potato, onions and cheese, seasoning each layer and finishing with potato. Fry gently until nearly cooked through and the underside is brown. Then turn over, putting a little dripping in the pan, and brown on the underside. Alternatively the top side can be browned gently under the grill.

Baked Stuffed Potatoes *Serves 4*

4 large potatoes   2 tbsp single cream
125g (4 oz) acid curd or cream cheese   salt and pepper
1 tsp made mustard   25g (1 oz) butter

Wash, scrub and dry the potatoes. Prick well all over with a fork to prevent the potatoes bursting in the oven. Place on a baking tray. Bake at 190°C (375°F), Mark 5 for 1½–2 hours or until the potatoes feel soft when pressed. Remove from the oven and cut in half lengthwise. Spoon out the insides into a bowl and mash with cheese, mustard and cream. Season to taste with salt and pepper, and pile the mixture back into the potato cases. Reheat in a hot oven, 220°C (425°F), Mark 7 for 15 minutes.

Onion Tart *Serves 4*

shortcrust pastry using
  100g (4 oz) flour (see Appendix 1)
2 large onions
25g (1 oz) butter
2 eggs

300ml (½ pt) single or soured cream
  or thin yoghurt
25g (1 oz) raisins
pinch of nutmeg
pinch of ginger
salt and pepper

Line a 20cm (8 in) flan tin with the pastry. Bake blind for 15 minutes at 200°C (400°F), Mark 6 (see Appendix 1). Slice the onions into rings and fry in butter until soft but not brown. Try to prevent the rings from breaking. Arrange in the cooked flan case. Beat the eggs with the cream or yoghurt, add the raisins, nutmeg, ginger, salt and pepper to taste; pour over the onions. Bake at 180°C (350°F), Mark 4 for 30 minutes or until the filling is set.

Leekie Pie *Serves 4*

This is a traditional Welsh recipe.

1 onion
25g (1 oz) butter
450g (1 lb) leeks
100g (4 oz) bacon rashers
salt and pepper

shortcrust pastry using 150g (6 oz) flour
  (see Appendix 1)
150ml (¼ pt) single cream
1 egg

Chop the onions and slice the leeks in 2½cm (1 in) pieces. Fry the onions in butter until soft, then add the leeks and bacon cut into small pieces, and cook until the leeks are soft. Cool slightly and season to taste. Line a 18–20cm (7–8 in) tart tin with just over half the pastry. Put in the leeks, onion and bacon. Beat the egg with the cream and pour over the leeks. Cover with the rest of the pastry and brush with a little beaten egg. Bake at 180°C (350°F), Mark 4 for 35–45 minutes until golden brown.

Creamed Parsnips *Serves 4*

The sweet flavour of parsnip was so much liked in the Middle Ages that it was often put in sweet pies and puddings with spices and honey. In this eighteenth century recipe it is served as a side dish.

500g (1 lb) parsnips
150ml (¼ pt) single or double cream
25g (1 oz) butter, softened

15g (½ oz) flour
salt and pepper

Peel the parsnips, quarter and boil in salted water until tender. Drain, slice and return to the saucepan with the cream, butter mixed with the flour and seasoning. Heat, stirring until the cream boils and the sauce thickens.

Salads

Potato Salad *Serves 4*

500g (1 lb) cold, cooked potatoes
1 tbsp finely grated onion
1 tbsp chopped mint
1 tsp caraway seeds

150ml (¼ pt) double or soured cream
 or thick yoghurt
2 tbsp lemon juice
salt and pepper

Cut the potatoes into small cubes. Mix with the onion, mint and caraway seeds. Stir in the cream or yoghurt, lemon juice, salt and pepper to taste until the potatoes are thickly coated.

Beetroot Salad *Serves 4*

350g (12 oz) cooked beetroot
150ml (¼ pt) thick yoghurt or soured cream

salt and pepper
1 tbsp chopped parsley

Slice or chop the beetroot. Mix with the yoghurt or cream, and add salt and pepper to taste. Sprinkle with chopped parsley.

Cucumber Salad *Serves 4*

1 cucumber
salt and pepper
1 small green pepper

150ml (¼ pt) thick yoghurt
1 tbsp chopped mint

Peel and slice the cucumber. Sprinkle with salt and leave for 30 minutes. Drain off liquid and sprinkle the cucumber with pepper. Chop the green pepper finely and add to the yoghurt. Stir in the cucumber. Pour into a serving dish and sprinkle with chopped mint.

Cream Cheese Cabbage Salad *Serves 4*

1 small white cabbage
1 red-skinned eating apple
1 tbsp finely chopped onion
125g (4 oz) acid curd or cream cheese

2 tbsp single cream
salt and pepper
1 tsp sugar
1 tbsp lemon juice

Shred or grate the cabbage finely, wash well and drain. Grate the apple without peeling. Mix with the cabbage and onion. Beat the cheese with the cream, salt and pepper, sugar and lemon juice. Pour over the cabbage and toss well.

6 Fish and meat

Fish

For an island nation, fish should be eaten more often than it is. During the Middle Ages it was a major part of the diet due to the many fish days decreed for religious and economic reasons: to mortify the flesh by abstaining from the pleasure of meat eating but also to save meat when it was scarce and to encourage the fishing industry. The rich ate a variety of sea and fresh water fish caught perhaps from their own mill ponds; the poor had only salt fish, the salting being essential to preserve it. After the abolition of compulsory fish days, fish was eaten less often and particularly the salt fish of the poor. Then at the end of the nineteenth century the 'fish and chip' shop arrived and fried fish became a cheap and national dish. However, fish can and should be cooked in many other ways besides frying and there is now a great variety of sea and fresh water fish, fresh, smoked or salted available to us.

Fish needs careful cooking to retain its subtle flavour and texture and to prevent it from becoming too dry, and it should be accompanied by an appropriate sauce. Milk and cream sauces are the traditional accompaniments.

Soles in Cream *Serves 4*

This recipe comes from Eliza Acton.

500g (1 lb) soles or plaice   salt and cayenne pepper
300ml (½ pt) single cream   2 tbsp lemon juice or white wine
pinch of ground mace   100g (4 oz) white grapes (optional)

Prepare the fish, and simmer in boiling, slightly salted water for 2 minutes. Lift out and drain. Place in a large pan or frying pan and cover with cream. Add the ground mace, salt and cayenne pepper and poach gently for 6–10 minutes until the flesh is cooked. Place the fish in the serving dish; stir the lemon juice or wine and the grapes into the cooking liquid and pour this over the fish. Serve immediately.

Fish Mousse *Serves 4*

225g (8 oz) cooked smoked haddock,   150ml (¼ pt) double or
  cod, salmon or tuna fish   soured cream or thick yoghurt
150ml (¼ pt) hot white coating sauce   salt and pepper
  (see p. 31)   1 egg white
15g (½ oz) gelatine   *To serve:* lemon wedges

Flake the fish, and mince or pound it very small. Stir into the hot white sauce. Dissolve the gelatine in 3 tbsp hot water (see Appendix 1), and stir into the fish mixture. If liked the mixture can be blended in a liquidizer. Stir in the cream or yoghurt and season to taste. Whip the egg white stiffly and fold in. Pour into a mould and chill until set. Unmould and serve with lemon wedges and a salad.

Fish Pie *Serves 4*

This a well known, traditional dish.

500g (1 lb) cod or haddock	1 hard boiled egg or 25g (1 oz) shelled prawns (optional)
300ml (½ pt) milk	500g (1 lb) cooked potatoes, mashed with butter and a little milk
300ml (½ pt) water	
25g (1 oz) butter	25g (1 oz) butter
25g (1 oz) flour	25g (1 oz) grated Cheddar cheese

Poach the fish in the milk and water combined until soft. Use the cooking liquid for making up the white sauce with the flour and butter (see p. 31). Mix the fish and the chopped, hard boiled egg or prawns into the sauce. Put into a buttered pie dish. Spread or pipe the soft mashed potato over the fish. Dot with butter and cheese if liked and bake at 180°C (350°F), Mark 4 for 45 minutes.

Baked Fish in Cheese Sauce *Serves 4*

500g (1 lb) fish steaks, fillets or small whole fish	4 tbsp dry cider
	2 tbsp breadcrumbs
600ml (1 pt) cheese pouring sauce (see p. 31)	25g (1 oz) butter

Place the fish in a buttered heatproof dish. Mix the cider into the cheese sauce and pour on top of the fish. Sprinkle with breadcrumbs and dot with butter. Bake at 180°C (350°F), Mark 4 for 30 minutes until the fish is cooked.

Trout with Cream and Fennel *Serves 4*

4 trout or herring	150ml (¼ pt) milk
flour	150ml (¼ pt) single or double cream
salt and pepper	
6 sprigs of fresh fennel or 2 tsp dried fennel	25g (1 oz) breadcrumbs
	25g (1 oz) butter

Rub the trout or herring in flour, salt and pepper and place in a buttered heatproof dish. Lay the fennel on top of the fish, pour in the milk, cover and bake at 200°C (400°F), Mark 6 for 20 minutes. Remove from the oven and stir in the cream. Sprinkle with breadcrumbs, dot with butter and brown under the grill.

Mackerel with Gooseberry Sauce *Serves 4*

Gooseberries are a traditional accompaniment to mackerel, popular since the eighteenth century. It is now a Cornish speciality.

250g (8 oz) fresh or tinned gooseberries   4 mackerel
25g (1 oz) melted butter   salt and pepper
150ml (¼ pt) double cream or 150ml   lemon juice
  (¼ pt) white coating sauce (see p. 31)   25g (1 oz) butter
pinch of nutmeg

If the gooseberries are fresh, prepare them by topping and tailing and cook gently in the melted butter until soft. It will not be necessary to cook the tinned gooseberries. Mash, sieve or liquidize and mix in the cream or the white sauce. Add the nutmeg and a little sugar if necessary, but the sauce should not be too sweet. Split the mackerel and bone it. Season with salt, black pepper and sprinkle with lemon juice. Dot with butter and grill for 10 minutes or until cooked. Serve with the hot gooseberry sauce.

Leek and Pilchard Pie *Serves 4*

This is a traditional recipe from Cornwall.

450g (1 lb) leeks   300ml (½ pt) clotted or double
water, milk   cream
225g (8 oz) fresh or tinned   shortcrust pastry using 75g (3 oz) flour
  pilchards   (see Appendix 1)

Wash the leeks, slice each one into two, but discard the coarser parts. Boil for a minute in a little milk and water. Drain. Put alternate layers of the leeks and pilchards into a buttered heatproof dish. Roll out the pastry and cover the leeks and pilchards with it. Brush with a little beaten egg or cream. Bake at 180°C (350°F), Mark 4 for 30 minutes. When cooked lift up the pie crust with a knife at the side and drain off the liquor. Heat the cream and pour into the pie.

Shellfish Cocktail *Serves 4*

a few lettuce leaves   2 tsp Worcester sauce
125g (4 oz) shrimps, prawns or tuna fish   2 tsp French mustard or
a small cucumber   tomato ketchup
150ml (¼ pt) thick yoghurt or   salt
  soured cream   1 tbsp chopped parsley
1 tbsp lemon juice   cayenne pepper

Shred the lettuce and place it in the bottom of 4 individual glass dishes. Prepare the shrimps or prawns or flake the tuna fish. Chop the cucumber finely. Mix the yoghurt or soured cream, lemon juice, Worcester sauce, mustard or tomato ketchup and a little salt to taste. Then stir in the fish and cucumber. Pour on top of the shredded lettuce and chill. Garnish with the chopped parsley and cayenne.

Meat

The Englishman is famed for his roast meats – beef, lamb, pork, venison, gamebirds and poultry. These were carved and served with rich sweet and sour sauces, with rice and cream puddings, with frumenty or savoury custard pies in the Middle Ages. Later on the accompaniments of Yorkshire Pudding, horseradish sauce and gravy for roast beef, onion sauce, mint sauce and redcurrant jelly for lamb, apple sauce and forcemeat stuffing for pork became more usual. Recipes for some of these traditional accompaniments are given in this chapter and in the chapter on sauces.

Often we have cold meat left over from our roast joint and this can then be used in meat loaves, mousses, pies, rissoles and potted meats. Milk, cream, cheese and butter are often essential components of these dishes and my selection includes recipes through the centuries.

Chicken Ramekins *Serves 4*

Adapted from an eighteenth century recipe.

225g (8 oz) cooked minced chicken
50g (2 oz) grated Cheshire
  cheese
25g (1 oz) breadcrumbs

2 eggs, separated
300ml (½ pt) single cream
salt and pepper
pinch of nutmeg

Beat the chicken, cheese and breadcrumbs together. Beat the egg yolks with the cream and stir in the chicken mixture. Add salt and pepper to taste and the nutmeg. Beat the egg whites until stiff and fold into the mixture. Pour into a buttered soufflé or pie dish, or individual ramekin dishes and bake at 180°C (350°F), Mark 4 for 45 minutes, or 30 minutes for the ramekins, until set and brown.

Chicken and Almond Mould *Serves 4*

A fourteenth century blancmange from the *Forme of Cury*.

The original blancmanges were made of white and mild flavoured meats such as chicken pounded to a pulp and mixed with almond milk, and rice. Over the centuries they gradually lost their meat base (see p. 83). The sugar in this recipe does not make it sweet, it only enhances the flavour. In medieval times sugar was very expensive and was used largely as a spice.

50g (2 oz) ground almonds
¼ tsp almond essence
1 tsp sugar
300ml (½ pt) milk
20g (¾ oz) ground rice
225g (8 oz) cooked minced chicken

300ml (½ pt) jellied stock
 (from the chicken if possible)
15g (½ oz) gelatine
salt and pepper
25g (1 oz) roasted almonds

Add the ground almonds, almond essence and sugar to the milk and bring
to the boil. Sprinkle on the ground rice and stir well. Heat until it thickens
and simmer for 10 minutes. Pound the chicken and add the stock, or purée
in a blender with the stock. Dissolve the gelatine in 3 tbsp hot water (see
Appendix 1) and add to the chicken. Then mix the chicken with the rice,
season to taste and pour into a mould. Chill to set. Turn out and decorate
with roasted split almonds.

Chicken in Yoghurt Sauce *Serves 4*

350g (12 oz) cooked chicken
1 onion
15g (½ oz) butter
1 tbsp cornflour
150ml (¼ pt) chicken stock

pinch of ginger
pinch of nutmeg
1 egg
150ml (¼ pt) thick yoghurt
salt and pepper

Chop the chicken into small pieces. Chop the onion finely and fry gently in
the butter until soft but not brown. Stir in the cornflour and chicken stock
to make a sauce. Add the chicken, ginger and nutmeg and simmer for 5
minutes. Beat the egg with the yoghurt and stir into the chicken. Heat until
the sauce thickens, and season to taste. Pour into a warm serving dish and
serve immediately.

Beef Breslaw *Serves 4*

(Or Beef Loaf) from Eliza Acton.

350g (12 oz) cold roast beef, minced
100g (4 oz) breadcrumbs
1 tbsp chopped parsley
1 tsp thyme

150ml (¼ pt) single cream
2 eggs
salt and pepper
pinch of nutmeg

Mix the beef with the breadcrumbs, parsley, thyme and cream. Beat the
eggs well and add to the mixture with salt and pepper to taste, and the
nutmeg. Put into a buttered heatproof dish or loaf tin and bake at 180°C
(350°F), Mark 4 for 45 minutes to 1 hour. Turn out and slice. Serve hot
with gravy, or yoghurt sauce (see p. 33). It is also good cold, served with
a mixed salad. This meat loaf can be made with other roast meat besides
beef.

Toad in the Hole *Serves 4*

Toad in the Hole may be thought to be a very commonplace dish, but in fact the baking of meat, fish and even small birds in a batter or custard pudding goes back to Roman times. Even Hannah Glasse gives a recipe for Pigeons in the Hole. Here is a nineteenth century recipe using pieces of meat rather than the usual sausages but of course sausages can be substituted.

100g (4 oz) plain or self-raising flour ⎫
pinch of salt   ⎪
1 egg   ⎬ basic batter
250ml (½ pt) milk   ⎭
25g (1 oz) beef dripping   500g (1 lb) beef steak,
salt and pepper   cut in thin strips

Sift together the flour and salt. Make a well in the centre and break in the egg. Add a little milk and beat the egg and milk into the flour. Gradually beat in the remainder of the milk until the mixture is light and frothy. Heat the dripping in a roasting pan and pour in a quarter of the batter to form a thin layer. Bake at 200°C (400°F), Mark 6 for 5 minutes so that it is lightly set. Fry the meat strips so that they are browned on both sides and lay on top of the batter. Season with salt and pepper. Cover with the remaining batter and bake for another 30–45 minutes until the batter is well risen and golden brown. Serve immediately with hot horseradish sauce (see p. 33) and a good gravy.

To make a plain Yorkshire Pudding, omit the meat, pour all the batter into the roasting tin at once and bake for 45–50 minutes.

Blanquette of Lamb *Serves 4*

This is a nineteenth century recipe.

350g (12 oz) cold lamb or veal   1–2 egg yolks
100g (4 oz) mushrooms   150ml (¼ pt) single or double cream
25g (1 oz) butter   1 tbsp lemon juice
450ml (¾ pt) white pouring sauce   salt and pepper
 (see p. 31)   *To serve:* chopped parsley, toast

Slice the meat very thinly and cut into strips. Slice the mushrooms and simmer in the butter for 10 minutes. Lay on top of the meat in the saucepan. Add the hot white sauce and reheat. Beat the egg yolks, cream and lemon juice together and stir into the sauce with the meat. Season to taste Heat but do not allow to boil. Serve garnished with chopped parsley and pieces of toast around the dish.

Lamb and Cheese Pie *Serves 4*

225g (8 oz) lean cooked lamb
shortcrust pastry using 150g (6 oz) flour
  (see Appendix 1)

2 tbsp chopped mint
125g (4 oz) acid curd cheese
2 tbsp single cream

Chop the lamb into small pieces. Line an 18cm (7 in) flan tin with just over half the pastry. Spread a layer of cheese on this, then the lamb mixed with the mint and finally another layer of cheese. Add the cream and cover the pie with the remaining pastry. Brush with a little beaten egg or milk and bake at 180°C (350°F), Mark 4 for 30–45 minutes.

Moussaka *Serves 4*

500g (1 lb) potatoes, cooked and sliced
  or 2 aubergines, sliced
oil
2 onions, sliced
25g (1 oz) butter
350g (12 oz) cooked minced lamb or
  beef
1 tsp mixed herbs

250g (8 oz) tomatoes, skinned
  (fresh or canned)
2 tbsp tomato purée
salt and pepper
150ml (¼ pt) thick yoghurt
1 egg
25g (1 oz) flour
50g (2 oz) grated Cheddar cheese
  (optional)

Fry the potatoes in oil until crisp, and lay in the bottom of a buttered pie dish. If aubergines are used, sprinkle the slices with salt and leave for 30 minutes. Drain off the liquid and fry in oil until soft. Place in the pie dish. Fry the onions in the butter until soft, add the minced meat, the herbs, tomatoes and tomato purée. Mix well together and add salt and pepper to taste. Spread on top of the potatoes or aubergines. Beat the yoghurt, egg and flour together, and season to taste. Pour over the meat. Sprinkle with the grated cheese. Bake at 180°C (350°F), Mark 4 for 30 minutes.

Pork Rissoles *Serves 4*

This is a very old medieval dish called Golden Apples, the 'apples' being made of minced pork, or pork and chicken, mixed with spices and sugar and fried crisp in batter. Half were coated in a batter containing finely chopped parsley so that they were green, the rest remained golden yellow.

Rissoles:
450g (1 lb) cold minced pork
½ tsp ginger
1 tsp mace
1 tsp sugar
salt and pepper
2 eggs, beaten

Batter:
1 egg
100g (4 oz) plain or self-raising flour
125ml (¼ pt) milk
salt
1 tbsp finely chopped parsley
fat for frying

Mix the pork, spices and sugar with salt and pepper to taste and bind together with the beaten eggs. Form into round rissoles. For the batter sift the flour, make a well in the centre and beat in the egg, milk and salt. Pour half the batter into another bowl and stir in the parsley. Dip each ball into one of the batters and fry immediately in smoking hot fat until golden. Drain off excess fat and keep warm while remainder are cooking. Serve straight away, for they should be very crisp.

Ham and Cheese Pasties *Serves 4*

This is adapted from a recipe by Robert May who suggests serving with grated cheese and sugar, but you can omit this if not according to your taste.

225g (8 oz) cooked minced ham	salt and pepper
125g (4 oz) grated Cheddar cheese	2 eggs, beaten
	500g (1 lb) cold boiled and mashed potatoes, turnips or parsnips
1 tsp sugar	
pinch of nutmeg	breadcrumbs
1 tsp made mustard	fat for frying

Mix the grated cheese with the ham and add the sugar, nutmeg, mustard, salt and pepper and one beaten egg. Mix in the cold potato, turnips or parsnips. Form into small balls, dip into remaining beaten egg and roll in breadcrumbs. Fry in deep hot fat until golden brown. Drain on kitchen paper to absorb excess fat and serve hot.

Cream Liver Pâté *Serves 4*

Adapted from Hannah Glasse's recipe.

500g (1 lb) calf's or lamb's liver	½ tsp nutmeg
	1 tsp thyme
2 onions, chopped	salt and pepper
25g (1 oz) butter	150ml (½ pt) single cream
2 tbsp chopped parsley	2 eggs, beaten
1 tsp ground cloves	50g (2 oz) breadcrumbs

Slice the liver thinly. Fry the liver and onions in the butter until lightly cooked. Mince; stir in the parsley, ground cloves, nutmeg, thyme, salt and pepper. Heat the cream and pour over the beaten eggs. Pour into the liver mixture and mix well together. Stir in the breadcrumbs and leave to stand for 10 minutes. Pour into a buttered loaf tin and cover with aluminium foil. Bake at 160°C (325°F), Mark 3 for 1 hour. Serve hot or cold.

Yoghurt Marinade for Grilled Lamb or Steak

The acid in yoghurt can be used to tenderize meat.

150ml (¼ pt) thin yoghurt salt and pepper
1 tbsp lemon juice 1 tbsp chopped fresh herbs
1 tbsp grated onion (optional)

Mix the ingredients, then add the meat pieces and cover well with the marinade. Cover marinading dish and chill for 3–6 hours, depending on the size of the pieces. Turn the meat frequently in the marinade. Take out and grill in the normal way.

Potted meat

It was the Elizabethans who began to preserve cooked meat under a layer of butter, developed as a way of preserving food for the long sea voyages undertaken in an age of discovery. Potted meat and fish became a fashionable dish amongst the rich. They were also part of the fare provided by coaching inns along with the pressed meats, brawns, cold hams; food was always available for the hungry traveller at any hour of the day or night. Now the deep freeze has to a large extent taken over from these traditional preserved foods, but we can still make and enjoy them. Potted meat is excellent served for a light lunch, for traditional breakfasts and high teas and of course as a starting course to dinner.

There are a host of recipes of course, but I give just one basic one to show the use of butter.

Potted Tongue

225g (8 oz) cooked tongue, ham or salt and pepper
  beef pinch of mace
100g (4 oz) clarified butter ½ tsp thyme
  (see p. 23) extra clarified butter for sealing

Mince the meat finely. Add the clarified butter and work it to a smooth paste. Season to taste with salt and pepper, add the mace and thyme. Press tightly into pots and chill. Reheat the extra clarified butter so that it melts and is warm, and pour over the tops of the pots to a depth of at least ½cm (¼ in). Cover with foil. It will keep in the refrigerator for a month, and for 3 months in the deep freeze.

7 Savoury cheese and egg dishes

Hard and soft cheeses have been used through the ages as essential ingredients of both savoury and sweet dishes from the 'cheese' cakes of Roman times down to the toasted and stewed cheeses popular in the seventeenth century. We are renowned as a nation for our splendid selection of hard and semi-hard cheeses. The semi-hard cheeses are only lightly pressed and are moister with a mild and slightly acid flavour. Such cheeses include Wensleydale, one of the famous and now only surviving Dale varieties developed in the monasteries of the Yorkshire dales in the Middle Ages; Caerphilly, whose small size enabled it to be taken down the mines as a convenient lunch packet by Welsh miners; and Lancashire whose crumbly nature makes it an excellent toasting cheese. The small-scale home-made cheeses such as Smallholder and Small Cheshire fall into this category, as they are only lightly pressed.

The hard pressed varieties include Cheshire which is reputed to be our oldest national cheese, first made in the twelfh century, and Cheddar, perhaps the most well known and most imitated, although nothing is the same as a fully mature Farmhouse Cheddar. Double Gloucester which is similar to Cheddar with a rich nutty flavour, and Derby, often impregnated with the juice of chopped sage leaves, are also hard pressed varieties.

Then there are the blue-veined cheeses: Blue Stilton of course, and the lesser known Blue Wensledale, Blue Cheshire and the Dorset Blue Vinney now difficult to obtain, but thought by many to be superior to Stilton.

These hard cheeses are ideal for cooking, Cheddar being the best general purpose cheese while Lancashire and Cheshire are excellent for toasting.

This chapter includes the old and traditional savoury dishes made with English hard cheese and also those made with soft home-made curd cheeses or cream. It contains more recipes using hard cheeses than other chapters, but of course you can use home-made hard cheese, the making of which is described in my book, *Making Cheeses*.

Toasted cheese

Toasted cheese became popular in Tudor times and was a national dish in Wales as the name 'Welsh Rabbit' (Welsh Rarebit, nowadays) suggests. The English version used toast soaked in wine rather than ale. Often the cheese was stewed in the wine first and then served with the hot toast. Later the use of toasted cheese was extended to other types of dishes, especially as a crisp savoury topping to some vegetables and also macaroni.

English Rabbit (Rarebit) *Serves 2*

Hannah Glasse gives this recipe.

2 thick slices of bread   125g (4 oz) Cheddar or
1 glass red wine   Cheshire cheese

Toast the bread on both sides, place in a heatproof dish and pour the red wine over it. Cut very thin slices of cheese and pile them on top of the bread. Place under the hot grill until the cheese is golden brown.

Welsh Rabbit (Rarebit) *Serves 2*

25g (1 oz) butter   1 tsp made mustard
2 tbsp ale (or milk)   125g (4 oz) grated Cheddar or Lancashire cheese
salt and pepper   2 slices toasted bread

Melt the butter in a heavy saucepan, add the ale, salt, pepper and mustard. Stir in the cheese to make a smooth, thick cream. Place the toast in a heatproof dish, pour the cheese over and place under a hot grill until the cheese is bubbly and brown. Serve immediately with a glass of red wine or ale.

Buck Rarebit

Make a Welsh Rabbit and serve a poached egg on each toast.

Roasted Cheese *Serves 2*

This makes an excellent supper dish for two, or the cheese toasts can be cut into fingers or triangles before baking and served as an appetizer or after dinner savoury.

2 tbsp milk   salt and cayenne pepper
25g (1 oz) breadcrumbs   75g (3 oz) grated Cheddar or Cheshire cheese
1 egg   2 slices buttered toast
1 tsp made mustard   1 tbsp chopped parsley

Heat the milk and soak the breadcrumbs in it. Beat the egg and mix with the breadcrumbs; season with mustard, salt and cayenne. Stir in the grated cheese. Spread on the buttered toast and roast in a hot oven, 200°C (400°F), Mark 6 for 20 minutes. Sprinkle with the chopped parsley and serve.

Macaroni Cheese *Serves 2*

Dr Kitchener gives this recipe in his book.

This unusual way of preparing macaroni cheese makes a delicious supper dish.

125g (4 oz) macaroni   125g (4 oz) grated Cheddar   25g (1 oz) butter
600ml (1 pt) milk   or Cheshire cheese   salt and pepper

Boil the macaroni in milk until soft. Stir in half the cheese, the butter and seasoning to taste. Heat so that the cheese melts but do not allow to boil; it will form a thick creamy sauce. Pour into a buttered, heatproof serving dish, sprinkle the remaining cheese on top and brown under a hot grill.

Omelettes

An Amlet *Serves 2*

This is Hannah Glasse's delicious creamy omelette. If liked it can be made without its sauce filling, or can be served with other fillings such as chopped ham or grated cheese.

Filling:

75g (3 oz) green beans or mushrooms	150ml (¼ pt) single cream
15g (½ oz) butter	salt and pepper
1 tbsp chopped parsley	pinch of nutmeg
	1 egg, beaten

Omelette:

150ml (¼ pt) single cream	salt and pepper
2 eggs, beaten	15g (½ oz) butter

Shred the beans finely and cook in fast boiling water until soft. Drain and fry in the butter with the chopped parsley. If mushrooms are used just chop and fry in butter. Pour in the cream and simmer for a few minutes, seasoning with salt and pepper and nutmeg. Remove from the heat, add the beaten egg and reheat gently so that the sauce thickens. Keep warm.

For the omelette, heat the cream and pour over the beaten eggs. Return to heat to thicken slightly. Season to taste with salt and pepper. Melt the butter in a large frying pan and when smoking hot pour in the mixture. Cook slowly until the underside is brown and the top is just setting. Pour the beans in their sauce onto one half of the omelette, fold over and serve.

Curd Cheese Soufflé Omelette *Serves 2*

50–75g (2–3 oz) acid curd cheese	salt and pepper
2–3 eggs, separated	15g (½ oz) butter

Beat the cheese with the egg yolks, add seasoning to taste. Beat the egg whites stiffly and fold in. Melt the butter in a large frying pan and when very hot pour in the mixture. Cook slowly until brown underneath, then grill top gently for 2 minutes.

Tarts and pies

Crustade Lombarde *Serves 4–6*

Adapted from a recipe in *Two Fifteenth Century Cookery Books.* This sweet and savoury custard pie (Lombardy Pie) was popular in the Middle Ages; it was served with the meat and fish course as a refreshing contrast in taste and texture. I include it in this section for this reason.

shortcrust pastry using 100g (4 oz) flour
  (see Appendix 1)
50g (2 oz) prunes
50g (2 oz) dates
300ml (½ pt) single cream

2 eggs, beaten
1 tbsp chopped parsley
  (optional)
1 tsp sugar
salt and pepper

Line a 20cm (8 in) tin with pastry and bake blind at 200°C (400°F), Mark 6 for 15 minutes (see Appendix 1). Remove stones from the dates and the prunes and chop finely. Heat the cream and pour over the beaten eggs. Stir in the parsley, sugar and seasoning. Arrange the dates and prunes in the pastry shell and pour in the custard mixture. Bake at 180°C (350°F), Mark 4 for 25–30 minutes. Serve with roast pork or baked ham.

Cream Cheese Tart *Serves 4*

This recipe is adapted from one given in the fourteenth century manuscript *The Forme of Cury*. The original recipe is called 'Tart de Bry'; Brie cheese was imported by England in the fourteenth century, but this recipe was probably also made with English soft cheese.

shortcrust pastry using 100g (4 oz)
  flour (see Appendix 1)
225g (8 oz) acid curd or cream cheese
4 tbsp single cream

pinch of ginger
1 tsp sugar
salt and pepper
2 eggs

Line a 20cm (8 in) flan tin with pastry and bake blind at 200°C (400°F), Mark 6 for 15 minutes (see Appendix 1). Blend cheese with cream, ginger, sugar, salt and pepper. Beat the eggs and then beat into the cheese. Pour into the pastry shell and bake at 180°C (350°F), Mark 4 for 30 minutes. To make tartlets roll out pastry and line small patty or tartlet tins. Do not bake blind but put cheese filling into tartlets straight away. Bake at 180°C (350°F), Mark 4 for 20 minutes. Serve hot or cold.

Green Cheese Tart

Green herb tarts were very popular in the Middle Ages. Use the above recipe, but omit the ginger and substitute 2 tbsp chopped parsley, 2 tbsp chopped marjoram and other chopped fresh herbs of your choice.

Cheese Pie *Serves 4*

A traditional recipe.

shortcrust pastry using
  100g (4 oz) flour (see Appendix 1)
25g (1 oz) butter

25g (1 oz) flour
250ml (½ pt milk)
1 tsp made mustard

75g (3 oz) grated
  Cheddar cheese
1 egg

Line a 20cm (8 in) flan tin with the pastry and bake blind at 200°C (400°F), Mark 6 for 15 minutes (see Appendix 1). Melt the butter, add the flour and cook over a low heat for 2 minutes. Remove from heat. Gradually add the milk, and heat, stirring all the time until the sauce comes to the boil and thickens. Stir in the mustard and grated cheese and remove from the heat. Beat the egg and stir into the sauce. Pour into the pastry case and bake at 180°C (350°F), Mark 4 for 30 minutes.

To make cheese tartlets line patty or tartlet tins with the pastry, fill with the sauce and bake for 20 minutes.

Elizabeth Raffald's Egg and Bacon Pie *Serves 4*

shortcrust pastry using
  150g (6 oz) flour (see Appendix 1)
125g (4 oz) streaky bacon
2 eggs

150ml (¼ pt) single, double or
  whipping cream
salt and pepper

Roll out the pastry and use just over half to line an 18cm (7 in) flan tin. Cut up the bacon and fry gently so that it is just cooked but not crisp. Arrange on pastry. Beat the eggs, retain a little for glazing and beat the remainder into the cream. Pour over the bacon. Cover the pie with remaining pastry and press edges together well. Brush with a little beaten egg and bake at 180°C (350°F), Mark 4 for 30 minutes. Serve hot or cold.

If liked, the pie can be cooked as an open tart without its top crust.

Cheese in other ways

Cheese Puffs *Makes about 24*

A recipe given by Eliza Acton.

Cream crust:
225g (8 oz) plain or
  self-raising flour
salt
75g (3 oz) grated cheese

150ml (¼ pt) whipping or double cream,
  approx.
50g (2 oz) butter

Sift the flour and salt, and mix in the cream to form a smooth dough. Turn out onto a floured board and knead well. Roll into a rectangle sufficient to enclose the portion of butter, put the butter on the lower half and fold the top half over, pressing the edges together. Put in a polythene bag or wrap in aluminium foil and chill for 15 minutes. Remove and roll out into a rectangle as thinly as possible, taking care that the butter does not come through the pastry. Fold in three, seal edges, wrap and chill. Roll out again and fold in three, turning the pastry so that the folds are at right angles to the first. Chill and repeat, this time sprinkling the pastry with grated cheese. Repeat until the cheese is well mixed into the pastry. Roll out to ½cm (¼ in) thickness and cut into rounds with a 5cm (2 in) biscuit cutter. Brush with beaten egg and milk and bake at 200°C (400°F), Mark 6 for 15 minutes. Serve hot as an appetizer or after dinner savoury.

Cream crust can be used with or without the addition of butter as a pastry lining for fruit tarts, meat pies, custard tarts and cheesecakes.

Cheese Soufflé *Serves 4*

50g (2 oz) butter	125g (4 oz) grated Cheddar or Cheshire cheese
50g (2 oz) flour	1 tsp made mustard
300ml (½ pt) milk	¼ tsp Worcester sauce
3 eggs, separated	salt and cayenne pepper

Melt the butter, add the flour and cook for 2 minutes, stirring all the time. Remove from the heat, gradually beat in the milk and heat, continuing to stir the sauce as it comes to the boil and thickens. Simmer for 2 minutes. This sauce is very thick and should leave the sides of the pan clean. Remove from the heat and beat in the egg yolks, cheese, mustard, Worcester sauce and salt and pepper. Beat egg whites stiffly and fold into the mixture gently. Pour into a buttered soufflé dish and bake at 190°C (375°F), Mark 5 for 45 minutes. The soufflé should be well risen and golden. Serve at once.

Mrs Beeton's Cheese Fondue *Serves 4*

4 eggs, separated	75g (3 oz) butter
125g (4 oz) grated Cheshire cheese	salt and pepper

Beat the egg yolks and then blend in the grated cheese and butter broken into small pieces. Season with salt and pepper. Whisk the egg whites stiffly and stir into cheese mixture lightly. Pour into a buttered soufflé dish and bake at 190°C (375°F), Mark 5 for 15–20 minutes until well risen. Serve immediately.

Potted Cheese

Hannah Glasse said of potted cheese: 'a slice of this exceeds all the cream cheese that can be made'.

500g (1 lb) Cheddar or Cheshire cheese	pinch of cayenne pepper
100g (3 oz) butter	½ tsp made mustard
2–3 tbsp sherry	clarified butter (see p. 23)

Grate the cheese and pound together with the butter. Add the sherry, butter and mustard. When well mixed, press down into pots, cover with warm clarified butter and then chill.

8 Hot puddings

The puddings of the English have been renowned since the end of the seventeenth century when the Frenchman, Misson, on visiting England wrote, 'Blessed be he that invented pudding, for it is a manna that hits the palate of all sortes of people'.

Black and white puddings made from animal blood or liver, suet, breadcrumbs and spices, stuffed into intestines and boiled, had been made for many years and in Tudor and Stuart times meatless versions with the addition of cream and eggs were developed but at first still boiled in intestines. Later the pudding cloth was invented, so that puddings could be made at all times of the year and not only at pig or sheep killing time. Also sugar became cheaper and larger quantities began to be used than had been hitherto. Puddings rapidly became part of the diet of both rich and poor and recipes abounded. For the rich there were delicious, light dessert puddings made from cream, eggs and flour; for the poor there were sweetened and unsweetened suet plum puddings, boiled in the same water as the meat and eaten as a first course so that appetites were somewhat appeased before the meagre meat course came.

Recipes were devised to bake the pudding in the bread oven, often in a pastry crust; these were known as pudding pies. Frequently pudding mixtures could be baked or boiled. There were rice and breadcrumb puddings, which had of course been made since medieval times, tansies, whitepots and batters, as well as the fruit tarts and pies. The meal was not complete without its pudding. Nowadays we no longer need or enjoy the traditional suet pudding, excepting perhaps if we work on a farm, and many do not bother to cook puddings at all. But children will always enjoy puddings and many of the hot puddings are extremely easy to make, can be baked in the oven at the same time as the meat and form a light but satisfying and nutritious ending to the meal.

Puddings

Quaking Pudding *Serves 4–6*

A delicious but light, boiled pudding dating back to the seventeenth century.

450ml (¾ pt) double or whipping cream	pinch of nutmeg
	pinch of salt
3 eggs, beaten	1 tsp rosewater (optional)
25g (1 oz) flour	75g (3 oz) sugar

Bring the cream to the boil and pour over the beaten eggs. Cool. Mix a little of this mixture with the flour to a smooth paste, then gradually beat in the rest with the nutmeg, salt, rosewater and sugar. Pour into a well-buttered pudding basin, cover with aluminium foil and steam for 1½ hours. Turn out and serve with a hot jam sauce or the traditional wine sauce (see p. 37). As the pudding is already rich you may wish to omit the melted butter in this sauce.

Hasty Pudding *Serves 4*

Adapted from Dorothy Hartley's recipe in *Food in England*. This quickly made pudding has been used in emergency for centuries.

1 tsp rosewater (optional)	25g (1 oz) butter
50g (2 oz) sugar	sugar
pinch of salt	cinnamon
600ml (1 pt) white coating sauce (see p. 31)	

Stir the rosewater, sugar and salt into the hot white sauce (see p. 31). Pour into a buttered pie dish, dot with butter and cover thickly with sugar and cinnamon. Put under a hot grill and leave until the sugar melts and becomes golden brown.

Rich Rice Pudding *Serves 4*

A rice pudding needs long, slow cooking for 2–3 hours. During the cooking time it should be stirred and milk added if it is too thick. This long cooking causes the milk to caramelize and gives the pudding its rich, creamy flavour and delicious golden skin. The method is ideal if you are using the oven for this length of time or if you have a solid fuel stove. If you are cooking something else at a higher temperature the rice pudding can be placed in a tin of water. However, if you wish to use the oven for a shorter time there is a quick method.

40g (1½ oz) pudding rice	½ tsp cinnamon
600ml (1 pt) milk	½ tsp vanilla essence
25g (1 oz) sugar	15g (½ oz) butter
1 egg, beaten	

Slow Method
Put the rice into a buttered heatproof dish and add the milk. Leave to soak for ½ hour. Stir in the sugar, cinnamon and vanilla essence and dot with butter. Bake at 140°–150°C (275°–300°F), Mark 1–2 for 2–2½ hours. Stir the pudding two or three times during cooking and if necessary add some more milk. After 1½–2 hours remove, cool for 10 minutes, stir in well beaten egg and then continue to bake for the required time.

Quick Method
Boil the rice in the milk with the sugar and then cook over a low heat until the rice is soft. Cool. Stir in the beaten egg, cinnamon and vanilla essence. Pour into a buttered pie dish, dot with butter and bake for 1 hour at 140°C (275°F), Mark 1.

The following recipes are adaptations of those in *Two Fifteenth Century Cookery Books;* these rich fruit and almond-flavoured rice pottages were served with the meat and fish at medieval meals. Now they make unusual and interesting rice puddings.

Medieval Fruit and Rice Pudding *Serves 4*

600ml (1 pt) milk or half milk and half single cream
50g (2 oz) ground almonds
½ tsp almond essence
25g (1 oz) sugar
40g (1½ oz) rice flour or semolina
2 tbsp honey
¼ tsp powdered ginger
25g (1 oz) chopped figs or dates
25g (1 oz) raisins

Put the milk, almonds and sugar into a saucepan and bring to the boil. Sprinkle in the rice flour or semolina and simmer until thick. Stir in the honey, ginger and dried fruit. Pour into a buttered pie dish and bake at 180°C (350°F), Mark 4 for 30 minutes until brown.

Apple and Rice Pudding (Rapeye) *Serves 4*

The addition of the beaten egg white turns this into an excellent, light, rice pudding soufflé.

250g (8 oz) apples
300ml (½ pt) milk
25g (1 oz) rice flour or semolina
½ tsp almond essence
50g (2 oz) sugar
1 tsp cinnamon
½ tsp ground cloves
1 egg, separated

Peel, core and slice the apples and cook in a little water until soft. Sieve or liquidize to a purée. Bring the milk to boiling point and sprinkle in the rice flour, almond essence and sugar. Simmer until thick. Mix with apple purée, egg yolk, cinnamon and ground cloves. Beat the egg white stiffly and fold into the mixture. Pour into a buttered pie dish and bake at 180°C (350°F), Mark 4 for 30 minutes until risen and golden brown.

Devonshire Whitepot *Serves 4*

This popular Tudor and Stuart dish was known as 'Devonshire' because of its rich cream content; it is a delicious version of the bread and butter pudding.

300ml (½ pt) cream, single, whipping or double
300ml (½ pt) milk
} or 600ml (1 pt) cream if you prefer

1 egg and 1 egg yolk
50g (2 oz) sugar
grated rind of ½ lemon
1 tsp rosewater or 1 tbsp brandy (optional)
pinch of salt
50g (2 oz) raisins
3 slices bread and butter
nutmeg

Beat the cream, milk, eggs, sugar, lemon rind, rosewater or brandy and salt together. Stir in the raisins. Pour into a buttered pie dish. Cut the bread into triangles and arrange on top of the cream mixture, buttered side uppermost. Sprinkle with nutmeg and bake at 180°C (350°F), Mark 4 for 40–45 minutes until the pudding is set and the top is crisp and golden.

Cream Toasts (Pain Perdu) *Serves 4*

This dish was introduced by the Normans in the Middle Ages then made by dipping slices of best white bread into egg yolk, frying and sprinkling with sugar. It still survives in one form or another as a nursery tea dish. Here is an eighteenth century recipe in which the bread is soaked in cream as well as egg.

1 egg or 2 egg yolks	grated rind of ½ lemon
150ml (¼ pt) single cream	4 slices white bread
25g (1 oz) sugar	clarified butter
½ tsp cinnamon	(see p. 23)

Beat the egg with the cream and sugar, add the cinnamon and lemon rind. Cut the bread into triangles and trim the crusts. Put in the cream mixture to soak for a minute, but do not allow to become too soggy. Fry in hot butter until crisp and golden; the use of clarified butter helps prevent the bread burning. Serve hot with sugar. If there is any egg mixture left it can be used for making a thin custard for serving with the toasts.

Little Almond Puddings *Serves 4*

A traditional recipe.

2 eggs, beaten	50g (2 oz) sugar
50g (2 oz) ground almonds	2 tbsp sweet sherry
½ tsp almond essence	300ml (½ pt) single cream or milk
grated rind and juice of ½ lemon	25g (1 oz) breadcrumbs

Mix all the ingredients together and pour into buttered ramekin dishes. Bake at 180°C (350°F), Mark 4 for 25–30 minutes until set and light brown. These are good served hot or cold.

Pippin Tansy *Serves 4*

The tansy was a form of early omelette, made with eggs and tansy leaves which gave it a somewhat bitter flavour. By the seventeenth century the tansy had become a sweet pudding, boiled, baked or fried, with the addition of breadcrumbs, sugar and cream and perhaps spinach juice to supply the green colour.

3 apples	½ tsp nutmeg
25g (1 oz) butter	50g (2 oz) sugar
3 eggs	a few drops green colouring
150ml (¼ pt) single cream	(optional)
50g (2 oz) white breadcrumbs	*To serve:* sugar

Peel and core the apples and cut in thick rings. Fry very slowly in butter until soft, but not coloured or burnt. Beat the eggs, cream, breadcrumbs, nutmeg and sugar and green colouring together and pour over the apples. Cook slowly until brown underneath, then grill top gently to brown. Serve sprinkled with sugar.

Tarts and pies

Tarts and pies have been enjoyed since the earliest times. The Romans made a soft flour and oil paste for wrapping around meat to seal it as it cooked. In northern Europe, lard and butter were used to form the paste which was then strong enough to form a container which could be filled. In medieval days pies of every description were eaten: open tarts made from pie shells which were baked empty first and were known as coffins or traps, closed pies with lids and little pasties which could be fried instead of being baked in the bread oven. The fillings were strange mixtures of sweet and savoury, meat, vegetables and dried fruit, spices, herbs and sugar. Pies with a 'shredded' meat filling were the forerunners of our minced meat pies, still traditional Christmas fare; these gradually lost their meat ingredient. Open tarts were filled with egg yolks and chopped meat or fish, or custard mixtures of eggs, cream or almond milk, with dried fruit, spices and sugar, or sometimes with fresh or ripened cheese. The sweet and savoury custard pies were served with poultry and game as an accompaniment (see p. 59). Fresh fruit was also put in pies and tarts. Raw fruit was considered unsafe for a long time, so fruit was cooked and pulped with sugar and spices and often mixed with cream to form the filling of Tudor and Elizabethan tarts.

Raspberry Tart with Cream *Serves 6*

Adapted from an eighteenth century recipe.

Other soft or stewed fresh fruit can be used instead of raspberries.

shortcrust pastry using 150g	50–75g (2–3 oz) sugar
(6 oz) flour (see Appendix 1)	450g (1 lb) fresh or frozen raspberries
1 egg, separated	150ml (¼ pt) single cream

Divide the pastry into two unequal halves, roll out the bigger half and line a 20cm (8 in) flan tin. Brush with some of the egg white and sprinkle with some of the sugar; this helps to prevent the pastry becoming soggy. Put in the raspberries with sugar to taste. Then roll out the rest of the pastry and cover the pie, leaving a small hole in the centre through which the cream can be poured later. Brush over the top of the pie with the rest of the egg white and sprinkle with sugar. Bake at 180°C (350°F), Mark 4 for 30 minutes or until the pastry is cooked. Beat the egg yolk with 25g (1 oz) sugar; boil the cream and pour over the egg. Then pour into the pie – a small kitchen funnel may be helpful. Return the pie to the oven for a further 5 minutes.

Damson Tart *Serves 6*

This tart can also be made with fresh or tinned cherries.

shortcrust pastry using 100–150g
  (4–6 oz) flour (see Appendix 1)
450g (1 lb) damsons or plums,
  fresh or drained, tinned

150ml (¼ pt) single or
  soured cream or thin yoghurt
1 egg
50g (2 oz) sugar

Line a 20–23cm (8–9 in) flan tin with the pastry and bake blind (see Appendix 1). Stone the damsons or plums and cut in halves or quarters according to size. Arrange decoratively in the pastry case. Beat the cream, egg, and sugar together and pour over the damsons. Bake at 180°C (350°F), Mark 4 for 30 minutes.

Apricot Pie *Serves 6*

shortcrust pastry using 100–150g (4–6 oz)
  flour (see Appendix 1)
100g (4 oz) dried apricots or 200g (8 oz)
  fresh or drained, tinned apricots
sugar to taste
½ tsp almond essence

2 eggs
50g (2 oz) sugar
300ml (½ pt) milk
For meringue topping (optional)
75g (3 oz) caster sugar

Line a 20–23cm (8–9 in) flan tin with pastry and bake blind (see Appendix 1). Soak the dried apricots overnight, then simmer in soaking water until soft. Skin and stone fresh apricots and simmer for a few minutes. The tinned apricots will not need cooking. Retain 1 or 2 apricots for decoration. Sieve or liquidize the rest and add a little sugar to taste and the almond essence. Beat the eggs with sugar, boil the milk and pour over the eggs. Stir into the apricot purée. Pour into the cooked pastry shell; slice the whole apricots and place in the filling in a decorative fashion. Bake at 150°C (300°F), Mark 2 for 30–40 minutes. Serve hot or cold.

This pie can be made with a meringue topping. Separate the eggs and make the filling with the egg yolks only. Cook the pie as before until the filling has set. Beat the egg whites until stiff and fold in 75g (3 oz) caster sugar. Pile on top of the pie and return to the oven. Bake at 130°C (250°F), Mark ½ until the meringue is set and brown.

A Doucet ('Something Sweet') *Serves 6*

A fifteenth century custard tart.

shortcrust pastry using 100–150g (4–6 oz) flour (see Appendix 1)
450ml (¾ pt) single, whipping or double cream

pinch of saffron (optional)
2 tbsp clear honey
2 eggs and 1 egg yolk

Line a 20–23cm (8–9 in) flan tin with pastry and bake blind (see Appendix 1). Bring the cream and saffron to the boil. Beat the eggs and honey together and pour on cream, beating well. Pour into pastry shell. Bake at 180°C (350°F), Mark 4 for 30 minutes or until set.

Chocolate Pudding Pie *Serves 6*

shortcrust pastry using 150g (6 oz) flour (see Appendix 1)
50g (2 oz) grated chocolate or 2 tbsp cocoa powder and 2 tbsp sugar
300ml (½ pt) single cream or milk
2 eggs
50g (2 oz) sugar

50g (2 oz) sponge biscuit crumbs
1 tsp orange flower water (optional)
½ tsp nutmeg
½ tsp cinnamon
pinch of ginger
Soured cream topping (optional)
150ml (¼ pt) soured cream

Line a 20cm (8 in) flan tin with the pastry, reserving some for a lattice top. Melt the grated chocolate or dissolve the cocoa powder in 2 tbsp boiling water. Stir into the cream or milk and bring to the boil. Beat the eggs with the sugar, add the biscuit crumbs, orange flower water, nutmeg, cinnamon and ginger. Stir in the boiled cream or milk and pour into the pastry case. Make a lattice work of pastry on top. Bake at 180°C (350°F), Mark 4 for 30–40 minutes until the pastry is cooked and the filling set. Serve hot with fresh or soured cream.

Soured cream makes an interesting topping: omit the pastry lattice work and when the filling has set pour over the soured cream. Return to the oven for a few minutes.

Pancakes

Pancakes and fritters of all kinds have been made for many centuries. There are many recipes for pancake batters: a very plain batter can be used for pancakes to be eaten immediately, but a richer mixture does remain crisper if the pancakes are to be kept hot and filled. Pancakes of the eighteenth century were particularly rich, using cream, many eggs, sack (sherry) and spices. These richer mixtures transform the common pancake into a regal dish.

Usually the dry ingredients are sifted into a basin, then a well is made in the centre and the eggs are put into the well with some of the liquid. The flour is gradually mixed in to make a very smooth paste and the rest of the liquid beaten in to the required consistency. The batter must be very well beaten to mix in plenty of air and so make the cooked pancakes light. It is not necessary to mix the batter some time before cooking as used to be thought; it will not improve it, but if it is mixed beforehand it should be kept as cold as possible. A batter should always be cooked quickly in hot fat or in a hot oven. Oil or lard is often recommended as it can be heated to a high temperature without smoking or burning.

Plain Pancake Batter *Makes about 8*

100g (4 oz) plain or self-raising flour	1 egg
	1 tbsp melted butter
pinch of salt	250ml (½ pt) milk

Sift the flour and salt together. Make a well in the centre of the flour and break in the egg, the melted butter and half the milk. Beat to a smooth creamy batter and then gradually beat in the rest of the milk. Grease a heavy frying pan with butter, and when very hot pour in 2 or 3 tbsp of the batter, tilting the pan so that the liquid coats the base of the pan thinly and evenly. Cook until the underside is golden brown. Toss or turn with a fish slice or spatula, and cook the other side until golden. Roll up, place on a hot dish and serve at once. Sweet dessert pancakes can be dredged with caster sugar and sprinkled with lemon juice, or spread with melted jam before rolling.

Rich Pancake Batter *Makes about 8*

75g (3 oz) plain or self-raising flour	2 tbsp melted butter
pinch of salt	250ml (½ pt) milk or half milk
25g (1 oz) sugar (optional)	and half single cream
2 eggs	butter for frying

Sift together the flour, salt and sugar if used. Stir in the eggs and melted butter and beat well. Add the milk or cream and beat again. Cook as for Plain Pancake Batter.

Apple Pancakes *Serves 4*

4 apples, peeled, cored and sliced	50g (2 oz) brown sugar
½ tsp cinnamon	250ml (½ pt) plain or rich pancake batter

Simmer the apple slices with cinnamon, sugar and a little water until soft. Cook the pancakes; put a little apple filling on each, roll up and sprinkle with sugar and cinnamon. Serve hot with fresh or soured cream.

Strawberry Cream Pancakes *Serves 4*

Other fruit can be used instead of strawberries.

150ml (¼ pt) double or whipping cream
250g (8 oz) fresh strawberries

250ml (½ pt) plain or rich pancake batter
caster sugar

Whip the cream until lightly stiff. Roughly chop the strawberries and fold into the cream. Cook pancakes and fill with strawberries and cream. Dredge with caster sugar.

Quire of Paper *Serves 4*

These very rich and paper-thin pancakes were popular in the eighteenth century and are similar to the French *crêpes* still eaten today. Instead of being rolled individually, the pancakes are piled on top of each other, the whole being cut into sections.

75g (3 oz) plain or self-raising flour
pinch of salt
15g (½ oz) sugar
2 eggs
250ml (½ pt) single cream

3 tbsp melted butter
½ tsp nutmeg
2 tbsp sherry
a little melted butter for frying
caster sugar

Sift the flour, salt and sugar into a bowl. Beat the eggs, add the cream and melted butter. Beat into the flour with the nutmeg to make a smooth batter. Add the sherry to make the consistency of thin cream. Heat a heavy bottomed frying pan and brush with melted butter. Pour in 1–2 tbsp of the batter and tilt the pan so that it runs evenly over the surface. Cook until lightly brown on both sides. There is no need to go on greasing the pan between pancakes as the mixture contains enough butter not to stick. Pile the pancakes evenly on top of each other, sprinkling each with caster sugar and keeping warm in the oven. Cut into wedges to serve.

Curd Cheese Blintzes *Serves 4*

250g (8 oz) acid curd cheese
1 egg, beaten
25g (1 oz) sugar
1 tsp vanilla essence
50g (2 oz) raisins

250ml (½ pt) plain or rich pancake batter
sugar
cinnamon
butter for frying

Mix the curd cheese with the beaten egg, sugar, vanilla and raisins. Cook the pancakes on one side only. Put the filling into the centre of the cooked side of the pancakes and fold over all the edges to make an envelope. Fry on both sides until golden. Drain. Sprinkle with sugar and cinnamon.

Fritters

Fritter batter is thicker than pancake batter as it must coat the food or bind it together. Foods of all kinds can be cooked in this manner: meat, fish, fruit, curds, herbs and even flowers. Fritter batters can be made from milk, milk and water, or water alone. Milk gives a soft solid batter, water a very crisp batter and milk and water a crisp outside with a soft inside. Choose the batter you want for a particular food or mixture. Fruit fritters are usually crisp and fluffy. The frying fat should be at least 2½cm (1 in) in depth, and for coated food possibly deeper, depending on the size of the pieces; it should be hot enough to seal the batter immediately. Only small amounts should be cooked at a time, and the fat allowed to reheat between batches. The fried food should be well drained on kitchen paper to absorb the surplus fat.

Fritter Recipe 1 (Suitable for fish, meat and vegetables)

100g (4 oz) plain or self-raising flour
  flour
pinch of salt

1 egg
1 tbsp melted butter
125ml (¼ pt) milk

Sift the flour and salt into a bowl. Add the egg and beat well, stir in the butter. Then add the milk gradually, beating all the time to make a smooth, thick consistency. Dip the food into the batter, and cook in the hot fat until golden brown.

Fritter Recipe 2 (Suitable for fruit)

100g (4 oz) plain or self-raising flour
pinch of salt
1 tbsp melted butter

125ml (¼ pt) water
2 egg whites

Sift the flour and salt into a bowl. Beat to a smooth paste with the butter and water. Just before using, beat the egg whites until stiff and stir into the batter lightly. Cook as for recipe 1.

Fritter Recipe 3 (Suitable for meat, vegetables and fruit)

100g (4 oz) plain or self-raising flour
pinch of salt
1 egg, separated

1 tbsp melted butter
125ml (¼ pt) milk, or milk
  and water

Sift the flour and salt. Add the egg yolk and melted butter and beat well. Beat in the milk to make a smooth paste. Just before using whisk the egg white and fold into the batter. Cook as for recipe 1.

Apple Fritters *Serves 4*

Apple fritters have been amongst the best loved through the ages.

4 good eating apples   1 tbsp brandy
sugar   125ml (¼ pt) fritter batter, recipe 2 or 3

Peel, core and cut the apples into rings about ½cm (¼ in) thick. Put in a dish, sprinkle with sugar and brandy and leave for several hours, turning the apples occasionally. Drain well and keep the marinading liquid. Make up the batter and beat in the marinading brandy with the milk. Dip the apple rings into the batter and fry in deep, hot oil for 3–4 minutes until golden. Drain on kitchen paper to absorb surplus fat and dredge with caster sugar before serving.

To make banana fritters marinate in sugar and rum.

Custard Fritters *Serves 4*

Eighteenth century recipe.

1 level tbsp flour   1 tbsp brandy
300ml (½ pt) milk or single cream   125ml (¼ pt) fritter batter,
2 egg yolks or 1 egg   recipe 1
pinch of nutmeg   pinch of ginger
pinch of salt   *To serve:* sugar, lemon juice

Blend the flour with a little cold milk. Warm the rest of the milk and gradually stir into the flour. Heat until the milk boils and the mixture thickens. Cool slightly and stir in egg yolks, nutmeg, salt and brandy. Pour into a buttered dish, place this in a pan of warm water and bake at 180°C (350°F), Mark 4 for 30 minutes or until set. Leave to become cold. Make up the batter and add the ginger. Cut the cold custard into pieces, dip into batter and fry in deep, hot oil. Drain and serve, sprinkled with sugar and lemon juice.

9 Cold desserts

It was during Tudor and Stuart times that milk and cream began to be used in great quantities to produce the rich and varied desserts of the banquet. The trifles, creams, syllabubs, snows, fools and junkets were all most beautifully made, and decorated and set out in a tempting array on the high table. In fact the term 'banquet' referred originally to just the final course of the feast at which these sweets and fruit desserts were served. Now of course we would not wish for such a selection at every meal, but for the special occasion or dinner party one of these cold desserts provides a perfect finale to an excellent meal. Most are simple, can be prepared in advance, and are light and smooth. And for those who do not wish for the rich cream content of some there are the chilled milk custards and blancmanges, the snows and mousses made with yoghurt and the soothing junkets.

Custards

The combination of egg and milk to make custard was discovered early in culinary history. The Romans combined eggs with other foods to thicken or bind in their fruit or vegetable, meat or fish *patinae,* or milk custards. In the Middle Ages both sweet and savoury custard mixtures were eaten. There were thick custards such as 'creme boylede' made from cream, egg yolks and sugar and coloured with saffron, cut into slices and decorated with flowers, or runny custards made from eggs and milk and poured over white bread to form a sort of early bread pudding. Eggs and thick cream made a filling for custard tarts; later the pastry case was removed and the custard baked by itself in a deep dish or in special custard cups.

There are many ways of cooking custards which produce slightly different results but they all require slow and careful cooking since too strong a heat causes the egg protein to curdle, so becoming stringy and hard. A custard to be turned out needs at least 4 eggs to 600ml (1 pt) of milk, so that it does not break. Egg yolks can be used instead of whole eggs; they give creamier custards, but then the number used must be increased. Two egg yolks are roughly equivalent to one egg.

Custards can be flavoured with grated nutmeg, cinnamon, vanilla, lemon or almond essence, or by infusing thinly cut strips of lemon rind in the milk for 30 minutes then removing before mixing with the eggs. To make chocolate custard, add 50g (2 oz) grated chocolate or 2 tbsp cocoa and 2 tbsp sugar dissolved in 2 tbsp boiling water to 600ml (1 pt) milk before heating. For a coffee custard add 2–3 tsp instant coffee powder dissolved in a little hot water to 600ml (1 pt) milk before heating.

Rich Boiled Custard *Serves 4*

This recipe dates back to the nineteenth century.

300ml (½ pt) milk
lemon rind, vanilla or almond
 essence

2 eggs and 2 egg yolks (or 3 eggs)
25g (1 oz) caster sugar
300ml (½ pt) single cream

Warm the milk and add the lemon rind to infuse. Strain. Beat the eggs with the sugar. Boil the milk and the cream and pour over the egg mixture. Return to the saucepan rinsed with cold water. Cook gently, stirring all the time, until the mixture thickens and it coats the spoon. Pour into a cool bowl, and add the flavouring preferred. Stir while cooling so that a skin does not form on the surface.

You can make this custard plainer or richer as liked by substituting milk or double cream for the single cream.

Steamed Custard *Serves 4*

600ml (1 pt) milk
flavourings

4 eggs
25g (1 oz) caster sugar

Warm the milk and flavourings. Beat the eggs with the sugar and pour in the warm milk. Pour into a buttered basin, cover with greased paper or aluminium foil and steam very gently for about 40 minutes until the custard is set. Turn out.

Baked Custard *Serves 4*

3–4 eggs
25g (1 oz) sugar

600ml (1 pt) milk
flavourings

Beat the eggs with the sugar. Warm the milk and pour over the egg mixture, stirring well. Add the flavourings. Strain the mixture into a buttered pie dish, stand in a tray of warm water and bake at 180°C (350°F), Mark 4 until just set, about 30 minutes. Remove the dish from the warm water to prevent further cooking. The custard can be cooked in individual dishes, in which case it will take a shorter time, about 20 minutes.

Orange Custards *Serves 4*

This is one of Elizabeth Raffald's recipes.

rind and juice of 1 orange (preferably Seville)
1 tbsp brandy
50g (2 oz) sugar

4 egg yolks
300ml (½ pt) single cream
300ml (½ pt) milk

Simmer the orange rind in water for 2 minutes, drain and mix with the brandy, orange juice, sugar and egg yolks. Boil the cream and the milk, add gradually to the egg mixture. Pour into buttered custard cups or ramekin dishes and place these in a baking tray of warm water. Bake at 160°C (325°F), Mark 3 for 20–25 minutes.

Baked Yoghurt Custard *Serves 4*

2 eggs	300ml (½ pt) thick or thin yoghurt
25g (1 oz) sugar	1 tsp vanilla essence
150ml (¼ pt) milk	ground cinnamon or nutmeg

Beat the eggs with the sugar. Mix the milk, yoghurt and the vanilla essence together and beat into the egg mixture. Pour into a buttered baking dish. Sprinkle with cinnamon or nutmeg. Stand in a tray of warm water and bake at 180°C (350°F), Mark 4 for 30 minutes or until set.

Snow Eggs *Serves 4*

This is an unusual seventeenth and eighteenth century recipe and looks very attractive. The cooking of the individual eggs takes some time so be prepared to do some other cooking while they are poaching.

3 eggs, separated	600ml (1 pt) milk	½ tsp cinnamon
50g (2 oz) sugar	½ tsp vanilla essence	

Beat the egg whites to a stiff snow. Add the sugar and continue beating until the mixture is shiny and stands in firm peaks. Boil the milk with the vanilla essence and cinnamon. When boiling, reduce the heat so that there are no bubbles and then place teaspoons of the egg white mixture carefully on the milk. You can cook 4 or 5 at once but they swell on cooking, so leave room. Poach gently for 4 minutes, turning once. Lift out each egg with a draining spoon and place on a clean cloth or kitchen paper to drain and cool. When all the mixture has been used, pour the hot milk onto the beaten egg yolks. Return to the saucepan and cook slowly until the custard thickens. Remove from heat and cool. Pour into a serving dish, arrange the poached snow eggs on top in a pyramid. Chill.

Caramel Cream *Serves 4*

4 tbsp sugar	3 eggs	450ml (¾ pt) milk
2 tbsp water	25g (1 oz) sugar	

Heat the sugar and water over a low heat to dissolve the sugar, stirring all the time. Boil, without stirring, until it turns a deep gold. Pour into 4 heated ramekin dishes or one large dish and tilt the dish quickly so that the sides are well coated. Beat the eggs with the sugar, heat the milk and pour into the egg mixture. Then pour this into the caramel coated dishes. Place in a tray of warm water and bake at 180°C (350°F), Mark 4 for 20–30 minutes until set. Chill and turn out to serve.

Creams

Sweet dishes made with cream became very popular in Tudor and Stuart times. The name 'cream' was given to a variety of mixtures from the simple cream made from a mixture of cream and flavouring, to creams thickened with eggs and flavoured, or mixed with fruit purée or jam. Later a cream was flavoured and set with gelatine. So creams, custards and fools all tend to overlap. Now a full cream usually refers to one flavoured with essences or liqueurs and set in gelatine, whereas the custard cream and flavouring or fruit mixtures are known as bavaroise or bavarian creams.

Chocolate Cream *Serves 4*

Elizabeth Raffald gives this recipe in her book.

50g (2 oz) chocolate, grated   300ml (½ pt) double or whipping
50g (2 oz) caster sugar   cream

Melt the chocolate in a little boiling water. Cool. Mix with the sugar and cream and whisk well. Pile into glasses. Chill and serve.

Burnt Cream *Serves 4*

This recipe was a speciality of several Cambridge colleges during the nineteenth century. It is a very rich but delicious pudding.

300ml (½ pt) single cream   caster or demerara sugar   3–4 egg yolks

Boil the cream and pour over the beaten egg yolks. Return to the saucepan and cook very slowly until the mixture thickens. Do not add sugar to the custard as traditionally this part is unsweetened. Pour into a buttered pie dish and chill overnight. Cover the cold cream with a ½cm (¼ in) layer of sugar. Put under a hot grill and leave until the sugar begins to caramelize. As soon as it is melted, remove and chill again before serving. Just tap the sugar crust with a spoon to crack it. This can be made in individual dishes, if liked.

The Countess's Cream *Serves 4*

Adapted from Eliza Acton's recipe.

500g (1 lb) chestnuts or   125g (4 oz) sugar
  350g (12 oz) unsweetened, tinned   150ml (¼ pt) milk
  chestnut purée   15g (½ oz) gelatine
lemon rind from ½ lemon   150ml (¼ pt) double or whipping
½ tsp almond essence   cream

Make a cut in the shell of each chestnut with a sharp knife and place in a saucepan, covering with cold water. Bring to the boil and cook for 2 minutes. Drain, peel and skin. Replace in boiling water and simmer for about 1 hour until tender. Strain and sieve to make a purée. Add the lemon rind, almond essence and sugar to the milk and simmer gently for 5 minutes to allow the flavour to infuse. Strain and cool. Dissolve the gelatine in 3 tbsp hot water (see Appendix 1) and stir into the milk, then stir the milk gradually into the cool chestnut purée. Whip the cream stiffly and fold into the chestnut mixture. Pour into one mould or separate glasses and leave to set.

Coffee Cream *Serves 4*

2 eggs	2–3 tsp instant coffee powder dissolved
50g (2 oz) sugar	in a little hot water
300ml (½ pt) milk	150ml (¼ pt) double or whipping cream
15g (½ oz) gelatine	

Beat the eggs and sugar together. Boil the milk and pour over the eggs. Return to the saucepan and cook gently until thick, stirring all the time. Cool. Dissolve the gelatine in 3 tbsp hot water (see Appendix 1). Stir the coffee essence into the cool custard and add the dissolved gelatine. Whip the cream until stiff and fold in lightly. Pour into a mould or glass dishes and chill to set.

Velvet Cream *Serves 4*

1½ tsp gelatine	1 wine glass sherry	300ml (½ pt) double or
75g (3 oz) sugar	juice of 1 lemon	whipping cream

Dissolve the gelatine in 2 tbsp hot water (see Appendix 1). Stir in the sugar until dissolved. Add the sherry and lemon juice. Leave to cool. Whip the cream until stiff and fold into the flavoured liquid gelatine. Pour into a mould or individual glasses and leave to set.

Fools and fruit creams

Fruit fools and creams date from the sixteenth and seventeenth centuries; they were based on the pulp of cooked fruits beaten together with cream and sugar. Eggs were sometimes beaten with the hot cream first to make a rich custard. Alas, nowadays a cornflour custard is often substituted for the cream, so depriving the dish of its original richness and lightness. Slightly acid fruits such as gooseberries, rhubarb or apricots make the best fools as their tartness combines well with the richness of the cream.

Gooseberry Fool *Serves 4*

250g (8 oz) gooseberries	150ml (¼ pt) double or whipping
sugar to taste	cream

Cook gooseberries in a little water until soft. Sieve or liquidize to a purée. Add sugar to taste. Leave to cool. Whip the cream and fold into the purée. Chill.

Raspberry Cream *Serves 4*

250g (8 oz) fresh or frozen raspberries   50g (2 oz) sugar
2 egg yolks   150ml (½ pt) single cream

Make a raspberry purée by sieving or liquidizing the raspberries. Beat the egg yolks with the sugar. Boil the cream and pour over the egg yolks. Return to the saucepan and heat slowly until thick. Cool and mix with raspberry purée. Pour into a serving bowl and chill.

Spiced Pear Cream (Chardewarden) *Serves 4*

This is an adaptation of the fifteenth century chardewarden (pulp of pears) which comprised warden pears simmered in wine or water, sieved, sweetened, spiced and thickened with egg yolk. I have added cream to make into a delicious pear cream, otherwise the recipe is as the original. Apples can be substituted for pears.

500g (1 lb) fresh or tinned pears   25g (1 oz) sugar   1 egg yolk
sweet white wine (optional)   1 tbsp honey   ½ tsp powdered ginger
150ml (¼ pt) single cream   ½ tsp cinnamon

If you use tinned pears you do not need to cook them. If using fresh pears, peel, core and slice. Simmer in a little white wine or water until soft. Cool slightly, add cream and sieve or liquidize to make a purée. Add sugar, honey and cinnamon and reheat to boiling point. Beat the egg yolk and stir in some of the pear purée. Return this to the rest of the purée and heat gently until thick. Pour into the serving dish and chill. Just before serving sprinkle with powdered ginger.

Snows, mousses and soufflés

Snows, mousses and soufflés all rely on the beaten egg white to give lightness and volume. Mousses and soufflés are relatively recent, although 'snows' made with beaten egg whites, cream, rosewater and sugar were part of the Elizabethan banquet. Yoghurt can be used in many of the recipes for those who do not want such a rich dessert. Of course yoghurt cannot be whipped, so that the dish will lose some of its lightness.

Apple Snow *Serves 4*

This is an adaptation of the traditional 'dish of snow'; later, apple pulp was added to give more body.

250g (8 oz) cooking apples 150ml (¼ pt) double or whipping cream
grated rind of ½ lemon 1 tsp rosewater (optional)
50g (2 oz) sugar 1 egg white

Peel, core and slice the apples. Cook slowly with a little water and lemon rind until soft. Add the sugar and sieve or liquidize to a purée. Cool. Whip the cream until lightly stiff and fold into apple purée, with the rosewater. Beat the egg white until stiff and fold in. Pour into one glass dish or individual serving dishes. Chill.

Banana Snow *Serves 4*

4 large bananas 50g (2 oz) sugar
juice of ½ orange 150ml (¼pt) double or whipping cream
150ml (¼ pt) thick yoghurt 1 egg white

Mash the bananas to a purée with the orange juice. Add the yoghurt and sugar and mix well. This can be done in a liquidizer. Whip the cream until lightly stiff. Beat egg white until stiff. Fold the cream and the egg white into the banana purée. Pile into serving dish. Chill.

Apricot Snow *Serves 4*

250g (8 oz) dried apricots 150ml (¼ pt) double or whipping
  or 500g (1 lb) drained tinned apricots cream or thick yoghurt
50g (2 oz) caster sugar 1 egg white
½ tsp almond essence *To decorate:* roasted almonds

Soak the dried apricots overnight and then cook until soft. Add sugar and simmer for 5 minutes. The tinned apricots will not require cooking. Sieve or liquidize to a purée. Add the almond essence. Cool. Whip the cream until lightly stiff and fold in; if yoghurt is used just fold in. Beat the egg white until stiff and fold in. Pour into glass dishes and chill. Decorate with roasted almond slivers.

Strawberry Mousse *Serves 4*

250g (8 oz) fresh or drained 150ml (¼ pt) double or whipping cream
  tinned strawberries or thick yoghurt
50g (2 oz) caster sugar 1 egg white
juice of ½ lemon *To serve:* strawberries, whipped cream
15g (½ oz) gelatine

Sieve or liquidize the strawberries and add the sugar and lemon juice. Dissolve the gelatine in 3 tbsp hot water (see Appendix 1) and add the strawberry purée. Leave in a cold place. When the mixture begins to set whip the cream until lightly stiff. Whip the egg white. Fold in the cream or yoghurt if used, and then the egg white. Pour into a mould and leave to set. This looks attractive if put into a ring mould. When turned out the centre can be filled with whole strawberries and whipped cream.

Lemon Soufflé *Serves 4*

grated rind and juice of 1 lemon
75g (3 oz) caster sugar
2 eggs, separated

15g (½ oz) gelatine
150ml (¼ pt) double or whipping cream
To decorate: chopped nuts, whipped cream

Prepare the soufflé dish first. Put 10cm (4 in) folded greaseproof paper around a 500ml (1 pt) soufflé dish, so that the paper stands 5cm (2 in) above the edge of the dish. Tie on securely. Mix the lemon rind and juice with the sugar and egg yolks and whisk over hot water until thick and fluffy. Dissolve the gelatine in 3 tbsp hot water (see Appendix 1) and add to the egg mixture. Leave this in a cold place until it begins to thicken and set. Whip the cream lightly and fold into the mixture. Beat the egg whites and fold in. Pour into the prepared soufflé dish and chill until set. Remove the greaseproof paper carefully. Decorate the sides with chopped nuts and the top with whipped cream.

Chocolate and Orange Soufflé *Serves 4*

15g (½ oz) gelatine
50g (2 oz) plain chocolate
  or 2 tbsp cocoa and 2 tbsp sugar
1 tsp vanilla essence
juice of 1 orange

50g (2 oz) caster sugar
2 eggs, separated
150ml (¼ pt) double or whipping cream
To decorate: nuts, whipped cream,
  grated chocolate

Prepare the soufflé dish as for the Lemon Soufflé above. Dissolve the gelatine in 3 tbsp hot water (see Appendix 1). Melt the chocolate or dissolve the cocoa and sugar in 2 tbsp hot water and add the vanilla. Mix the orange juice, sugar and egg yolks and whisk over hot water until it is thick and fluffy. Then add the gelatine and chocolate. Leave to cool until it just begins to thicken and set. Whip the cream and fold into the mixture. Beat the egg whites and fold in. Pour into a soufflé dish and chill until set. Remove the paper and decorate with nuts, whipped cream and grated chocolate shavings.

Blancmanges

Blancmanges date back to the Middle Ages although their nature was slightly different to what we know today. Then they were a strange medieval mixture of meat and sweet things. White-coloured meats such as pork or chicken were cooked and ground to a pulp in a mortar, then combined with almond milk, boiled rice and sugar. Sometimes part of the blancmange was coloured red or yellow to contrast with the usual colour 'white'. Blancmange made with fish was eaten on fast days. In Elizabethan days an alternative version was made, a meatless blancmange of cream, sugar and rosewater thickened with eggs. And by the seventeenth and eighteenth centuries English blancmanges had become a kind of jelly made with isinglass or hartshorn jelly, milk, cream or beaten egg whites and flavoured with almonds. In the nineteenth century arrowroot was imported from the West Indies and soon recipes were created for American or West Indian blancmange made with boiling milk and arrowroot. This was the precurser of the modern cornflour blancmange.

Good Common Blancmange *Serves 4*

Eliza Acton gives this recipe in her book.

450ml (¾ pt) milk	15g (½ oz) gelatine
grated rind of ½ lemon	150ml (¼ pt) single or double
½ tsp almond essence	cream
75g (3 oz) sugar	2 tbsp brandy (optional)

Warm the milk and add the lemon rind to infuse. Leave for 30 minutes and strain. Add the almond essence and sugar. Dissolve the gelatine in 3 tbsp hot water (see Appendix 1) and add to the milk. Add the cream and stir well. Then mix in the brandy gradually. Pour into a mould and chill to set.

Contrast this recipe with another Victorian recipe below, using cornflour.

Almond Blancmange *Serves 4*

Given by Dorothy Hartley in *Food in England.*

3 level tbsp cornflour	75g (3 oz) sugar
600ml (1 pt) milk	1 tsp almond essence
2 bayleaves	roasted split almonds

Mix the cornflour with a little cold milk to a smooth paste. Heat the rest of the milk with the bayleaves and when boiling remove the bayleaves and pour the milk over the cornflour; add sugar and return to the saucepan. Bring to the boil and simmer for 2–3 minutes stirring all the time. Add the almond essence. Pour into a mould, and when cold stick with split almonds.

Flummery and frumenty

Flummery is very similar to blancmange. The early traditional flummery was an oatmeal dish: fine oatmeal was steeped in water, strained and boiled with continuous stirring until it was almost solid. In the seventeenth and eighteenth centuries the name was used for a form of jelly made with spiced cream or ground almonds. It was eaten as part of the second course with cream or wine, and for special occasions it was set in special moulds to make party pieces. There are directions in the old cookery books for making flummery fish in a fish pond, flummery eggs in the hen's nest and flummery eggs and bacon. Nowadays the name seems to be used for any acid and starch-based jelly using various combinations of cream, fruit, wine and gelatine.

Frumenty is often confused with flummery, maybe because of the similarity of names, but it is made from whole wheat, boiled until it is swollen and soft and then mixed with cream, spices, currants, egg yolks and brandy. It can probably claim to be our oldest national dish, going back to Neolithic farmers who boiled their roughly ground wheat to make primitive pottages and gruels. In medieval times frumenty was an accompaniment to meat dishes such as venison or porpoise on fish days for the rich; for the poor it was probably a meal in itself. Later it became a dinner sweet or a special festive dish to be eaten during the twelve days of Christmas or at Easter time. In fact in some parts of the country it is still traditionally eaten on such occasions.

Frumenty is made from hulled or pearled wheat which has the outer husk removed. The wheat must be cree'd or stewed so the grains swell and burst and a thick glutinous mess is produced. When cold it forms a firm jelly in which the burst grains of wheat are embedded. This process is described in the recipe. If liked pearl barley can be used instead. Frumenty can be eaten for breakfast as an English version of the Swiss muesli, or as a good supper dish, or as a hot or cold dessert.

Orange Flummery *Serves 4*

15g (½ oz) gelatine
50g (2 oz) sugar
150ml (¼ pt) orange juice
1 tbsp orange flower water
  or sweet white wine

300ml (½ pt) double or whipping cream
2 oranges, peeled and sliced
caster sugar

Dissolve the gelatine in 3 tbsp hot water (see Appendix 1) then stir in the sugar until this has dissolved. Add the orange juice and orange flower water or wine. Leave to cool. Lightly whip the cream and fold into the gelatine mixture. Pour into a mould and chill to set. Turn out and serve surrounded with the orange slices sprinkled with a little sugar.

Frumenty *Serves 4*

125g (4 oz) hulled or pearled wheat
600ml (1 pt) milk
50g (2 oz) currants, raisins or sultanas
50g (2 oz) sugar or honey

1 tsp cinnamon
1 egg or 1 tbsp flour mixed with
  2 tbsp milk (optional)
To serve: cream, nuts,
  chopped fresh fruit

Put the wheat grains in a bowl, cover with cold water and leave to soak overnight in a warm place. Boil the wheat until soft and thick, stirring so that it does not stick to the saucepan. This is the process of cree'ing. If liked a pressure cooker can be used to speed up the process. Now add the milk and cook until the frumenty is the consistency of thick porridge. Stir in the dried fruit, sugar or honey and cinnamon. A beaten egg or a little flour mixed with milk can be added to thicken the mixture. Serve hot or cold with cream, nuts, chopped apples or bananas.

Syllabubs, trifles and junkets

The name 'syllabub' derives from the old French champagne Sille, and the word 'bub' which was common Elizabethan slang for a bubbling drink; the wine Sille was mixed with frothing cream to make a Sille Bub. Syllabubs were of two kinds: the liquid syllabubs which were a favourite drink of the Tudors and Stuarts, and the more solid everlasting syllabubs of the banquet course. The most simple syllabub was one in which milk, warm from the cow, was milked directly into a bowl of sweetened and spiced cider, wine or beer; the new milk naturally formed a froth as the fine jet issued from the udder, the acid of the wine reacted to give a light curd on top and a delicious whey underneath. There are many recipes for this 'syllabub under the cow' in the old recipe books, sometimes known as 'Hatted Kit'. Sometimes dairies were turned into elegant rooms where rich country ladies took their friends to drink syllabubs warm from the cow. 'Wooden cows' became available to imitate the action of the real cow. In Georgian times a hand whisk was used to froth the cream and wine together and produce the whipped cream syllabubs. These were served in special syllabub glasses so that the creamy whip could be clearly seen above the clear liquid below. Now syllabubs are regaining their popularity as a perfect finish to a dinner party menu. They are rich but light and their attractiveness lies not least in their simplicity of preparation by the hostess.

Recipes for trifles are recorded as far back as the sixteenth century cookery books; again, they have changed considerably in nature over the centuries to the present day trifle. The English trifle is perhaps the best known of our traditional desserts, but unfortunately the 'modern' version of sponge cakes soaked in fruit juices or encased in jelly and covered with cornflour custard and cream is a poor parody of what a truly excellent and intoxicating dish it can be.

Junket has been a popular sweet dish since medieval days. It was served especially on holidays, feast days and at fairs hence the term 'junketing' associated with country revels. The first junket was a special form of green cheese, broken and drained, the curd mixed with sugar and rosewater. Indeed the word 'junket' is thought to come from the Norman French word *jonquet*, the little rush basket used for draining the curd. Later on the junket was not broken or drained but served with cinnamon or nutmeg, and fresh or clotted cream.

Syllabubs

Whipt Syllabub *Serves 4–6*

Hannah Glasse suggests that any wine, cider or lemon or orange whey, sweetened to taste can be used for this whipped liquid syllabub.

300ml (½ pt) red wine   150ml (¼ pt) sherry
25–50g (1–2 oz) sugar   grated rind and juice of 1 orange
300ml (½ pt) double cream   75g (3 oz) sugar

Sweeten the red wine with the sugar and pour into individual glasses. Mix the rest of the ingredients together and whip well, then pile onto the red wine in the glasses and serve immediately.

Lemon Syllabub *Serves 4–6*

Elizabeth Raffald gives this recipe for a liquid syllabub in her book.

300ml (½ pt) double cream   75g (3 oz) caster sugar
300ml (½ pt) sweet white wine   grated rind and juice of 1 lemon

Mix all the ingredients together and stand for 2 hours. Whisk well and pile into glasses. Chill overnight; the syllabub will separate to give a creamy froth on top and a clear liquid below.

Everlasting Syllabub *Serves 4*

A nineteenth century recipe.

grated rind and juice of 1 lemon   75g (3 oz) caster sugar
1–2 tbsp brandy   300ml (½ pt) double cream
3 tbsp sherry
Leave the lemon rind to soak in the lemon juice, brandy and sherry for 2–3 hours. Strain over the sugar and stir until dissolved. Pour in the cream and beat until stiff. Pile into individual glasses and chill.

Orange and Lemon Syllabub *Serves 4*

This is a non-alcoholic version of syllabub.

juice of 2 oranges and 1 lemon or juice of   75g (3 oz) caster sugar
  1 orange and 150ml (¼ pt) lemon whey   300ml (½ pt) double cream

Mix all the ingredients together and whisk well. Pile into individual glasses and chill well.

Cider Syllabub *Serves 4*

This is Robert May's recipe.

150ml (¼ pt) dry or sweet cider   pinch of nutmeg
75g (3 oz) sugar   300ml (½ pt) double cream

Beat all the ingredients together until light and foamy. Chill well.

Trifles

Orange Trifle *Serves 4–6*

8 large macaroons   2 eggs
  (see Appendix 1)   25g (1 oz) sugar
4 tbsp brandy or sherry   300ml (½ pt) single cream or milk
1 tbsp orange juice   150ml (¼ pt) double or whipping
2 oranges, peeled and thinly   cream
  sliced   glacé cherries

Arrange the macaroons in a glass serving dish and pour over the brandy or sherry and the orange juice. Leave to soak. Arrange the orange slices on top of the macaroons. Beat the eggs with the sugar. Boil the cream or milk, pour over the eggs and return to the saucepan. Heat gently until the custard thickens. Cool, then pour over the macaroons and oranges. Whip the cream until stiff and pile on top of the custard. Decorate with glacé cherries. Chill.

Eliza Acton's Excellent Trifle *Serves 6–8*

This trifle is made with syllabub.

4 large macaroons (see Appendix 1)   *Syllabub:*
8 sponge biscuits (see Appendix 1)   rind and juice of ½ lemon
1 wine glass wine or sherry   1 tbsp brandy
1 wine glass brandy   1 tbsp sherry
600ml (1 pt) Rich Boiled Custard   25g (1 oz) caster sugar
  (see p. 77)   150ml (¼ pt) double cream

                                     To decorate: candied peel,
                                       ratafia biscuits

Arrange the macaroons and sponge biscuits in a glass serving dish and pour wine and brandy over them. Allow to soak. Make up the boiled custard as described on p. 77 and leave to cool. Pour over the macaroons and sponge biscuits. Make up the Everlasting Syllabub as described on p. 87 and pile on top of the custard. Decorate with candied peel and ratafia biscuits.

If liked this can be converted into a non-alcoholic trifle. Soak the macaroons and sponge biscuits in 2 wine glasses fruit juice. Top the trifle with an Orange and Lemon Syllabub (p. 87) using half the quantities.

Swiss Cream *Serves 4–6*

600ml (1 pt) single cream	40g (1½ oz) rice flour
grated rind and juice of 1 lemon	50g (2 oz) sugar
piece of cinnamon	8 macaroons (see Appendix 1)
2 eggs yolks	*To decorate:* candied peel

Warm the cream with the lemon rind and cinnamon and infuse for 30 minutes. Beat the egg yolks with the rice flour and sugar; strain the hot cream over this mixture. Heat gently until thick and then cool. When cold add the lemon juice. Put half the macaroons in a glass serving dish, pour in half of the cream, put in the rest of the macaroons and then the rest of the cream. Decorate with candied peel. Chill.

Tipsy Cake *Serves 6–8*

Sponge cake:	*Custard:*
50g (2 oz) plain flour	2 eggs
pinch of salt	25g (1 oz) caster sugar
2 eggs	300ml (½ pt) milk
75g (3 oz) caster sugar	*Topping:*
150ml (¼ pt) white wine	150ml (¼ pt) double or whipping cream
1 tbsp brandy	50g (2 oz) split roasted almonds or 100g (4 oz) fresh or frozen raspberries or strawberries

Make up the sponge cake 3 or 4 days in advance so that it is dry enough to soak up the alcohol. Sift the flour and salt. Whisk the eggs and sugar together until thick and creamy. Fold in the flour gently and pour into a 15cm (6 in) greased and floured cake tin. If you have an ornamental sponge mould use that. Bake at 180°C (350°F), Mark 4 for 30 minutes.

Put the sponge cake in a shallow serving dish and prick all over with a fork. Pour over the wine and brandy and leave to soak. Spoon up any surplus and pour over the cake again. Make up the custard (see p. 77). and cool. Whip the cream until stiff and pile on top of the sponge cake. Decorate with roasted almonds, or with the soft fruit. Pour the cold custard sauce around the base of the cake and serve.

Junkets

Fresh Cheese in Cream *Serves 2*

This comes down to us from the seventeenth century.

50g (2 oz) ground almonds pinch of salt
½ tsp almond essence 1 tsp rosewater
50g (2 oz) sugar 1 tsp ground ginger
600ml (1 pt) milk 1 rennet tablet or 1 tsp rennet essence

To serve: single or double cream, wafers

Add the ground almonds, essence, sugar, salt, rosewater and ginger to the milk. Heat to 38°C (100°F) and stir in the rennet tablet dissolved in water or the rennet essence. Cover and leave in a warm place for 1 hour. Prepare a mould in a muslin-lined colander as explained on p. 16. Ladle thin slices of the curd into this mould and leave to drain for a few hours. Remove the fresh cheese from the mould and chill. Save the whey. Serve with cream and wafers (see p. 107). The whey makes a particularly delicious spicy drink; it should be served very cold.

Devonshire Junket *Serves 4*

600ml (1 pt) milk 3–4 tbsp brandy
25g (1 oz) sugar 150ml (¼ pt) clotted cream
1 junket rennet tablet or 1 tsp rennet essence cinnamon or nutmeg

Heat the milk and sugar together to 38°C (100°F). Dissolve a junket rennet tablet in warm water. Pour the brandy into a glass serving dish and mix in the milk. Add the dissolved rennet or rennet essence and stir well. Cover and leave in a warm place to set. When set, place in the refrigerator to cool. Spread the surface with clotted cream (if it is stiff, mix with a little fresh cream) and sprinkle with cinnamon or nutmeg.

Tea Cream *Serves 4*

Although called a 'cream', this is really a tea-flavoured junket. It was popular in the early eighteenth century, but later was superseded by the less subtle and richer Coffee Cream (see p. 80).

300ml (½ pt) milk 50–75g (2–3 oz) sugar
10g (¼ oz) China tea 300ml (½ pt) single cream
 1 rennet tablet or 1 tsp rennet essence

Warm the milk, tea and sugar together to not more than 71°C (160°F) and leave to infuse for 10 minutes. Strain and add the cream. Warm to 38°C (100°F) and pour into a glass serving dish. Stir in the rennet tablet dissolved in a little warm water or the rennet essence. Cover and leave in a warm place to set. Chill and serve with wafers (p. 107).

10 Ice cream

Iced sweets are reputed to have been made for thousands of years, as far back as 3000 B.C. by the Chinese. But it was not until the thirteenth or fourteenth century A.D. that the recipes were brought to Italy and they gradually spread throughout Europe to Britain and then to America. The first recipes for ice cream in Britain appeared in the eighteenth century. Ice was cut from frozen rivers in the winter months and stored in ice houses for cooling and freezing in the summer. The early ice creams were made in special pewter containers, an inner bowl for the cream and an outer one for the mixture of broken ice and salt, similar to ice cream makers still in use today.

The first ice creams were mixtures of cream, sugar, sieved fruit or jam; later, frozen custard and water ices were also used. Now of course ice creams are made on a commercial scale and consist of a variety of ingredients which include cream or vegetable fat, milk powder, sugar, emulsifier, stabilizer and flavourings (dairy ice cream must contain milk fat). Unfortunately many people have only eaten the commercial variety and do not know the delights of home-made ice cream which has an inimitable taste and texture of its own. It is extremely easy to make and very nutritious and children can be persuaded to eat egg custard when it is presented in this way!

Ice cream can be made at home in the freezing compartment of the refrigerator or in a freezer. There are small electric ice cream makers available. These fit into the refrigerator or freezer and usually consist of a shallow container with a paddle which rotates continuously while the mixture is freezing. However, these are relatively expensive and very good ice cream can be made without them as long as the mixture is removed and beaten once or twice during the freezing time to prevent the formation of large ice crystals. The old-fashioned churn for large quantities of ice cream, with an inner metal container and an outer wooden bucket is not easily available now and requires large amounts of ice and coarse freezing salt.

There are several basic recipes for home-made ice cream. These are:

1 whipped cream and sugar
2 boiled custard made with milk and eggs or cornflour, plus whipped cream
3 rich boiled custard made from cream and eggs

Gelatine and beaten egg whites can be added to any of these recipes, plus flavourings and fruit purées. Air must be incorporated into the mixture at some stage otherwise it will freeze hard or have a very coarse texture with large ice crystals. Including whipped cream and beaten egg whites, and also whipping the mixture during freezing all help to improve the texture and prevent the formation of large ice crystals. Gelatine acts as a stabilizer and holds the ice crystals apart while sugar prevents crystallization and of course provides sweetness. Ice cream mixtures always taste very sweet and overflavoured when unfrozen, and seem less sweet to the taste buds when freezing cold. But too much sugar can prevent freezing. Cream gives richness and smoothness, the butterfat helping to prevent crystallization. Fruit and nuts delay the freezing process, so they are usually added when the mixture is half frozen.

For good results follow these basic steps:

1 Always chill the mixture or ingredients thoroughly before freezing.

2 Freeze quickly: if using a refrigerator turn the control of the freezer compartment to the coldest setting at least half an hour before. This fast freezing will help to prevent the formation of large ice crystals. After the mixture has frozen, turn the control back to normal so that the ice cream does not become too hard.

3 Freeze the mixture in freezing trays, polythene or other suitable flat-bottomed containers. The bottom of the container should be in contact with the freezing surface.

4 Freeze the mixture until it is half-frozen, when there is a solid layer around the edges but still a soft centre. The time that the mixture takes to freeze depends on a number of factors: the temperature of the freezing compartment, the type of container used, the quantity in any one container and the particular recipe. It will freeze slower in a refrigerator, faster in the freezer, and faster in a metal container than in polythene.

5 Put into a chilled bowl and beat with a wooden spoon, hand whisk or electric beater at slow speed until smooth. Replace in containers and continue freezing.

6 The mixture can be removed again for a further beating before it is finally frozen. Other ingredients are often added at the final beating stage, such as whipped cream, beaten egg white or chopped fruit and nuts.

7 When the mixture has frozen it can be left in the same container or placed in metal or plastic moulds. Special ice cream or bombe moulds with lids are available but rectangular polythene boxes or cake tins are suitable. Spoon in the soft but frozen mixture and smooth down with the back of a spoon. To unmould, loosen the top edge of the ice cream with a knife, dip the mould quickly in warm water and dry, and then turn the ice cream out onto the serving dish.

8 Ice cream can be stored for up to one month in a freezer, but will be too hard to eat if taken directly from the freezer. It should be thawed out slowly in the refrigerator for several hours depending on the type of container, quantity made and type of mixture.

Various flavours

Vanilla Ice Cream 1 *Serves 4*

300ml (½ pt) double or whipping cream   1 tsp vanilla essence
50g (2 oz) sifted icing sugar   1 egg white, beaten (optional)

Whip the cream until lightly stiff. Stir in the icing sugar and vanilla essence. Pour into a freezing tray. Freeze for 30–45 minutes until the ice cream has frozen around the edges. Put into a chilled bowl and stir gently until smooth. Fold in the beaten egg white if used. Return to the washed, dried tray. Freeze for 2 hours until firm.

Vanilla Ice Cream 2 *Serves 4–6*

1 egg   2 tsp vanilla essence
100g (4 oz) sugar   150ml (¼ pt) double or whipping
300ml (½ pt) milk   cream

Beat the egg with the sugar. Boil the milk and pour over the egg mixture. Return to the saucepan and cook gently until it thickens. Pour into a cool bowl, stir in the vanilla and leave to cool. The custard can be made with cornflour or custard powder using 1 tbsp powder to 300ml (½ pt) milk. Pour into a freezing tray and freeze until the mixture has frozen around the edges. Pour into a chilled bowl and beat until very smooth. Whip the cream until lightly stiff and fold into the ice cream. Return to the tray and freeze for 1½–2 hours or until firm.

Vanilla Ice Cream 3 *Serves 4*

2 eggs   300ml (½ pt) single cream
75g (3 oz) sugar   2 tsp vanilla essence

Beat the eggs with the sugar. Boil the cream and pour over the egg mixture. Return to the pan and cook gently until the mixture thickens. Pour into a cool bowl, stir in the vanilla and leave until cold. Pour into a freezing tray. Freeze for 30–45 minutes until the ice cream has frozen around the edges. Put into a chilled bowl and beat until smooth. Return to tray and freeze for 2 hours until firm.

Vanilla Milk Ice *Serves 4*

A less rich vanilla milk ice can be made by substituting milk for the single cream in the above recipe. Boil the milk for a few minutes to concentrate it before adding to the eggs. As the fat content of the milk is lower, larger ice crystals are formed more easily in this mixture. One can add 15g (½ oz) gelatine dissolved in 3 tbsp hot water (see Appendix 1) to the custard to help stabilize the mixture. Also it should be beaten at least twice during the freezing process to prevent the formation of large ice crystals.

The preceding four recipes can be used as a basis for other varieties, such as:

Almond Ice Cream

Add almond essence instead of vanilla. At the final beating before freezing, stir in 25g (1 oz) roasted, chopped almonds.

Chocolate Chip Ice Cream

Stir in 50g (2 oz) grated plain chocolate before final freezing.

Coffee Ice Cream

Substitute the vanilla by 2–3 tsp instant coffee powder dissolved in a little boiling water and then cooled.

Fruit Ice Creams

Stir in 75–100g (3–4 oz) chopped or sliced, fresh or drained, tinned fruit before final freezing.

Apricot Ice Cream *Serves 4*

This is adapted from the first English recipe published for the making of ice cream, by Hannah Glasse.

125g (4 oz) dried apricots or 250g (8 oz) fresh or drained, tinned apricots	50g (2 oz) sifted icing sugar ½ tsp almond essence 300ml (½ pt) double or whipping cream

Soak the dried apricots overnight, then simmer in the soaking water until soft. Skin and stone the fresh apricots and simmer for a few minutes. Sieve or liquidize the apricots and add the sugar and almond essence. Beat the cream until lightly stiff. Fold in the fruit purée and pour into a freezing tray. Freeze for 30–45 minutes or until the mixture has frozen around the edges of the tray. Pour into a chilled bowl and beat gently until smooth. Return to the washed and dried tray. Freeze for 2 hours or until firm.

Strawberry Ice Cream *Serves 4–6*

Adapted from Eliza Acton's recipe.

250g (8 oz) fresh strawberries 125g (4 oz) sugar 300ml (½ pt) milk	300ml (½ pt) double cream juice of 1 lemon

Crush the strawberries slightly and cover with sugar. Leave to stand for

3–4 hours, then sieve or liquidize to a purée. Mix milk with the double cream and then stir in the strawberry purée and the lemon juice. Pour into a freezing tray and freeze until the mixture has frozen around the edges. Pour into a chilled bowl and beat until very smooth. Return to the tray and freeze for 2 hours or until firm.

Brown Bread Ice Cream *Serves 4*

A popular Victorian ice cream.

2 eggs, separated	1 tsp vanilla essence or 1 tbsp rum
100g (4 oz) caster sugar	50g (2 oz) wholemeal breadcrumbs
300ml (½ pt) single cream	

Beat the egg yolks with 75g (3 oz) sugar. Boil the cream and pour over the egg mixture. Return to the saucepan and cook gently until the mixture thickens. Pour into a cool bowl, add the vanilla or rum and leave until cold. Pour into a freezing tray and freeze until the mixture has frozen around the edges. Meanwhile gently grill the breadcrumbs with the rest of the sugar until crisp and brown. Cool. Pour the half-frozen ice cream into a chilled bowl and beat until smooth. Whisk egg whites until stiff and fold into mixture with breadcrumbs. Return to tray and freeze until firm.

Blackcurrant Ice Cream *Serves 4*

Blackberries can be used instead of blackcurrants.

250g (8 oz) fresh or frozen blackcurrants	caster sugar
150ml (¼ pt) double or whipping cream	2 tsp gelatine

Simmer the prepared currants in a little water until soft. Add sugar to make slightly oversweet. Sieve or liquidize and if necessary add more water to make up to 300ml (½ pt) purée. Dissolve the gelatine in 2 tbsp hot water (see Appendix 1) and add to the purée. Leave until cold and beginning to thicken. Lightly whip the cream and fold in the fruit purée. Freeze without stirring.

Frozen mousses and iced soufflés

Mousses and iced soufflés are rich ice cream mixtures which do not require beating during freezing. The particular ingredients in the mix prevent the formation of large ice crystals. Frozen mousses are made from egg yolks, sugar, flavouring and cream; iced soufflés are made from egg whites, syrup, flavouring and cream.

Orange Mousse *Serves 4*

150ml (¼ pt) orange juice   2 egg yolks
100g (4 oz) caster sugar   150ml (¼ pt) double or whipping cream

Heat the orange juice and the sugar in a double sauce pan until the sugar dissolves. Beat the egg yolks until thick and pale in colour. Add to the orange mixture and beat over hot water until the mixture thickens. Cool in a pan of cold water, whisking occasionally. Whip the cream until lightly stiff and fold into the cold orange mixture. Freeze.

Frozen Yoghurt Soufflé *Serves 4*

15g (½ oz) gelatine   50g (2 oz) icing sugar
150ml (¼ pt) thick yoghurt   150ml (¼ pt) double or whipping cream
½ tsp vanilla essence   1 egg white

Dissolve the gelatine in 3 tbsp hot water (see Appendix). Leave to cool. Stir into the yoghurt with the vanilla essence and icing sugar. Beat the cream until lightly stiff. Fold into the yoghurt. Beat the egg white until stiff and fold in. Pour into a freezing tray and freeze without stirring, until firm.

Mint Soufflé *Serves 4*

125g (4 oz) caster sugar   pinch of salt
4 tbsp chopped fresh mint   2–3 drops green vegetable
2 egg whites   colouring (optional)
150ml (½ pt) double or whipping cream   *To decorate:* grated chocolate,
                                         fresh mint

Make a syrup with the sugar and 4 tbsp water and boil for 5 minutes. Pour over the chopped mint, cover and stand for 1 hour. Strain through a muslin cloth and heat the syrup again. Beat the egg whites until stiff, and pour in the hot syrup, beating all the time until the mixture is like a thick meringue. Cool by standing in a saucepan of cold water and whisking occasionally. Whip the cream until lightly stiff. Add the salt and colouring to the meringue mixture and fold in the cream. Pour into a mould and freeze without stirring. Unmould and decorate with grated chocolate and sprigs of fresh mint.

Iced Raspberry Soufflé *Serves 4*

Strawberry purée can be used instead of raspberry.

125g (4 oz) fresh, frozen or drained,   125g (4 oz) sugar
   tinned raspberries   2 egg whites
2 tsp lemon juice   150ml (¼ pt) double or whipping
sugar to taste   cream

Make a purée by sieving or liquidizing fruit and add lemon juice and sugar to taste. Chill. Make a syrup with the sugar and 4 tbsp water. Boil for 5 minutes. Beat egg whites until stiff, then pour in the hot syrup slowly, beating all the time until the mixture is like a thick meringue. Cool by standing in a saucepan of cold water and whisking occasionally. Whip the cream until lightly stiff. Beat the raspberry purée into the meringue mixture, then fold in the whipped cream. Pour into a mould and freeze without beating. Unmould before serving.

Bombes

Bombes, which became popular at the end of the nineteenth century, are usually made of two different ice creams, one layer used as a lining and the other as the centre, but sometimes they have three or four layers including mousse or iced soufflé mixtures. The first bombes were made in the shape of a bomb, in a spherical mould made in two halves. Nowadays bombe moulds which you can buy are basin-shaped with a fitting lid. You can improvise with heat-resistant glass pudding basins, or plastic bowls with lids.

When moulding the bombe, the mould should be thoroughly chilled first. Spoon in the outside coating layer which should be frozen but still soft enough to smooth down into an even layer. Use the back of the spoon to mould it evenly around the sides and base. Put the mould in the freezer to harden this layer a little, then add the second layer or centre. The ice creams can be ones that thaw at the same rates, or the centre can be one that softens more quickly than the outside. When the mould is full, level the top, cover and put back in the freezer. To serve, the bombe should be taken out of the freezer 1–2 hours in advance and unmoulded straight away. It can then be left in the refrigerator to thaw slowly before serving.

Once you have made several ice cream mixtures of various types you can experiment with bombe mixes, and the choice is entirely yours, according to taste. Here are some suggestions for suitable combinations:

Vanilla ice cream (p. 94) and raspberry soufflé (p. 97) in the centre
Almond ice cream (p. 95) and apricot ice cream (p. 95) in the centre
Chocolate chip ice cream (p. 95) and orange mousse (p. 97) in the centre

The size of mould will depend entirely upon the quantity of ice cream. The volume of each ice cream mix can be measured just before freezing which will indicate approximately the size of mould needed. Any surplus mixture can of course be frozen separately.

11 Bread and cakes

Through the ages breads have been enriched with milk and butter as well as honey, eggs and spices; up to the eighteenth century there was little distinction between the enriched breads and cakes, although 'cakes' were often of a smaller size, served as an accompaniment to wine or ale. Later huge 'cakes' appeared made with large quantities of flour, dried fruit, butter, cream, eggs and sugar. Such cakes had to be raised with a good amount of 'ale-yeast' to prevent them sagging under the quantity of dried fruit. However, by the eighteenth century, eggs began to be used more as a raising agent, often beaten for more than an hour at a time, and cakes became smaller again. In the nineteenth century when the taking of afternoon tea became so popular, recipes for cakes abounded and included the pound cake using a pound of flour, a pound of butter, a pound of sugar and a pound in weight of eggs. There were also sponge cakes in which the egg whites were beaten separately from the yolks and then folded into the flour mixture, and soda cake in which carbonate of soda was used to help the cake rise.

Yeast cookery

Plain and preferably strong flour should be used. Strong flour contains more gluten than an ordinary cake flour and so rises better with the yeast. Fresh or dried yeast can be used, dried yeast has the advantage that it can be kept for several months as long as the tin is airtight. It is easily available in most grocery shops and supermarkets and is easy to use. Fresh yeast does not keep very long but it may give a better taste to your bread and rise more quickly. 15g (½ oz) dried yeast is equal to 25–30g (1 oz) fresh yeast.

All yeast needs the right conditions to grow – warmth and moisture – so all ingredients and equipment should be warm. The yeast should be creamed or dissolved first. Cream the fresh yeast with a little warm milk or water and sugar, using a teaspoon. Dried yeast can be sprinkled onto warm liquid containing the dissolved sugar. Leave for 10–15 minutes in a warm place until it becomes frothy and the yeast begins to work. The yeast should then be mixed into the flour with the rest of the liquid and the dough kneaded to distribute the yeast throughout and also strengthen the flour gluten. In most mixtures the dough should be smooth and not at all sticky, so more flour can be added as needed. Put the dough in a clean greased bowl, cover with a damp cloth and leave to rise in a warm place until it is double in size. It can then be knocked down, kneaded lightly, fruit and other heavier ingredients added and the dough shaped. Proving for another 20–30 minutes allows the dough to rise again so that it doubles in size. It can be then baked in a very hot oven.

Milk Loaf

450g (1 lb) plain flour
1 tsp salt
25g (1 oz) butter
15g (½ oz) fresh yeast or 2 level tsp dried yeast

250ml (½ pt) warm milk, approx.
1 tsp sugar
1 egg, beaten

Sift the flour and salt and rub in the butter. Cream or dissolve the yeast in a little of the warm milk and the sugar and leave for 15 minutes until frothy. Make a well in the centre of the flour, pour in the yeast and the beaten egg, mix in the rest of the milk gradually to give a soft dough, then knead on a floured board. Leave to rise in a warm place until double its size. Knead again and divide into two, shape each into an oval loaf and put in 500g (1 lb) greased and floured tins. Prove for 30 minutes until the dough has doubled in size, brush with milk and bake at 230°C (450°F), Mark 8 for 10 minutes and then at 190°C (375°F), Mark 5 for 35–40 minutes.

Milk Rolls *Makes 12*

Make the dough using the Milk Loaf recipe above. After the first rising, divide the dough into 12 small pieces and shape into round balls, long finger rolls, crescents, twists or plaits. Place on a greased baking sheet and leave to prove for 30 minutes. Brush with milk or beaten egg and bake at 230°C (450°F), Mark 8 for 15–20 minutes.

Kentish Huffkins *Makes 3*

These are thick, flat, oval cakes with a hole in the middle. Make the basic Milk Loaf dough, but omit the egg. After the first rising, shape into 3 oval cakes with a hole in the middle. Leave to prove and bake at 230°C (450°F), Mark 8 for about 30 minutes. After baking, wrap in a tea cloth so that the huffkins keep a soft crust.

Cornwall Splits *Make 15*

Make up the basic Milk Loaf dough, but omit the egg. After the first rising shape into about 15 rounds. Prove and brush with milk. Bake for 15 minutes at 230°C (450°F), Mark 8. Cut through, spread with butter and clotted cream and serve hot.

Rich Fruit Loaf

Adapted from Hannah Glasse's recipe.

225g (8 oz) plain flour
pinch of salt
50g (2 oz) butter
75g (3 oz) sugar
1 tsp cinnamon

½ tsp nutmeg
15g (½ oz) fresh yeast or
  2 level tsp dried yeast
125ml (¼ pt) warm single
  cream or milk, approx.

1 egg, beaten
150g (6 oz) currants
  and sultanas soaked in
  brandy or water
25g (1 oz) candied peel

Sift the flour and salt together, and rub in the butter finely. Mix in the sugar and spices. Cream or dissolve the yeast in a little of the warm cream or milk and 1 tsp sugar and leave in a warm place until frothy. Make a well in the centre of the flour and add the beaten egg, yeast mixture, and the rest of the cream gradually to give a soft dough. Leave to rise in a warm place until double in size, and fold in the dried fruit which has been well drained and tossed in flour to dry it, and the chopped peel. Put in a greased, floured cake or loaf tin and leave to rise again until double in size. Bake at 230°C (450°F), Mark 8 for 10 minutes, and then 180°C (350°F), Mark 4 for 40–45 minutes.

Wiggs *Makes 16*

Originally wedge-shaped, these small breakfast buns became known as wiggs. In the seventeenth century they were commonly eaten with tea and coffee for the lighter breakfast meal which had come into fashion. This is an eighteenth century recipe.

450g (1 lb) plain flour	½ tsp ginger
pinch of salt	25g (1 oz) fresh yeast or 4 level tsp dried yeast
75g (3 oz) butter	150ml (¼ pt) warm milk
75g (3 oz) sugar	1 egg, beaten
½ tsp nutmeg	1 tbsp sherry (optional)

Sift the flour and salt together and rub in the butter until it is like fine breadcrumbs. Mix in the sugar and spices. Cream or dissolve the yeast with a little of the warm milk and 1 tsp sugar and pour into a well in the flour with the beaten egg, the rest of the milk and sherry if used. Mix to a soft dough and then knead on a floured board until the dough is smooth. Leave to rise until the dough has doubled in size, then knead again lightly and divide into about 16 pieces. Shape into round buns and place on a greased, floured baking tray, leaving room between each for spreading. Leave to prove for 30 minutes. Brush with milk or beaten egg and bake at 230°C (450°F), Mark 8 for 15 minutes until brown.

Girdle breads

Crumpets (Pikelets) *Makes 22*

'Pikelet' was the name given to this girdle-cooked flour and milk mixture, a Midland form of the Welsh word meaning 'pitchy bread'. The Anglo-Saxon word 'crumpet' was also used for this type of bread.

15g (½ oz) fresh yeast or 2 tsp dried yeast	450g (1 lb) plain flour
600ml (1 pt) warm milk	1 tsp salt
1 tsp sugar	pinch of bicarbonate of soda

Cream or dissolve the yeast with a little of the warm milk and the sugar, leave to become frothy. Sift the flour and salt and make a well in the middle. Pour in the yeast mixture and the rest of the milk. Beat very well for 5 minutes, then cover and leave to rise in a warm place for 1 hour. Dissolve the bicarbonate of soda in a little warm water and add to the flour mixture, beat well and leave to rise for another hour. Grease a girdle or thick frying pan and heat until moderately hot. Grease crumpet rings (you can use large, round metal biscuit cutters if you cannot obtain crumpet rings) and place on girdle. Pour in the mixture to cover the bottom of each ring to a depth of ½ cm (¼ in). Cook until set on top and the bubbles burst, turn over and cook on the other side. To serve, toast in the usual way and eat with plenty of butter.

Muffins *Makes 15*

Muffins are made from a similar, but slightly stiffer flour and milk mixture than Crumpets, and can be enriched with egg and butter. It is only comparatively recently that the muffin man has disappeared from our streets, ringing his bell to anounce 'hot muffins' at teatime.

15g (½ oz) fresh yeast or 2 tsp dried yeast
250ml (½ pt) warm milk
1 tsp sugar
25g (1 oz) butter
1 egg
450g (1 lb) plain flour
1 tsp salt

Cream or dissolve the yeast in a little warm milk and add the sugar. Melt the butter in the rest of the milk and beat in the egg. Sift the flour and salt together, make a well in the centre and pour in the yeast and milk and egg mixture. Mix well and knead to a soft, smooth dough. Cover with a damp cloth and leave until it has doubled in size. Roll out to 1 cm (½ in) thickness and cut with a large biscuit cutter. Cook the muffins on a greased girdle or heavy frying pan over a moderate heat, turning over when risen and slightly brown. Alternatively they can be baked on a greased tray in a hot oven 230°C (450°F), Mark 8. Bake for 5 minutes and when slightly brown, take out of the oven, turn over and bake for another 5 minutes. To serve, toast, pull apart and put in a knob of butter. Muffins are never cut, only pulled apart; they will be like a honeycomb inside. Keep warm, and turn over so that the butter soaks into both halves.

Bread and cakes without yeast

Bread and scones have been made with sour milk and buttermilk for many years especially in the north. Bicarbonate of soda is used as a raising agent and needs an acid to help it release all its gas which causes the dough to rise. Cultured buttermilk or yoghurt provide this acidity. Baking powder contains bicarbonate of soda and an acid ingredient already mixed together.

Soda Bread *Makes 2*

450g (1 lb) plain flour   2 level tsp bicarbonate of soda
1 tsp salt   300ml (½ pt) thin yoghurt
25g (1 oz) butter   or cultured buttermilk, approx.
1 tsp sugar

Sift the flour and salt and rub in the butter. Add the sugar and bicarbonate of soda and mix in the yoghurt or buttermilk lightly. Shape into 2 loaves and put in 2 greased loaf tins. Bake at 230°C (450°F), Mark 8 for 25–30 minutes.

Parkin

A traditional Yorkshire recipe.

225g (8 oz) self-raising flour   100g (4 oz) oatmeal
½ tsp salt   1 tbsp black treacle or golden syrup
1 tsp mixed spice   100g (4 oz) butter
1 tsp cinnamon   100g (4 oz) soft brown sugar
½ tsp ginger   150ml (¼ pt) thin yoghurt or milk
1 tsp bicarbonate of soda   1 egg, beaten

Sift the flour, salt, spices and bicarbonate of soda into a bowl. Add the oatmeal and make a well in the centre. Heat the treacle, butter and sugar together until the butter melts. Pour into the well with the beaten egg and the yoghurt. Stir the mixture well and pour into a greased 20cm (8 in) cake tin. Bake at 160°C (325°F), Mark 3 for 1 hour or until a knife stuck into the centre of the cake comes out clean. Parkin can be stored for a week without cutting. Slice and spread with butter.

Yoghurt Fruit and Nut Loaf

100g (4 oz) butter   ½ tsp cinnamon
225g (8 oz) self-raising flour   ½ tsp mixed spice
100g (4 oz) brown sugar   150ml (¼ pt) thick yoghurt
150g (6 oz) dried mixed fruit,   or cultured buttermilk
  or chopped dates   1 tbsp black treacle or golden syrup
25g (1 oz) chopped nuts   1 tsp bicarbonate of soda

Rub the butter into the flour. Add the sugar, dried fruit and spices. Warm the yoghurt or buttermilk, add the treacle and bicarbonate of soda and mix well until frothy. Pour into the flour mixture, stir in well and put in a greased cake or loaf tin. Bake at 180°C (350°F), Mark 4 for 45 minutes.

Mrs Beeton's Honey Cake

100g (4 oz) sugar
150ml (¼ pt) soured cream or
 thin yoghurt

225g (8 oz) self-raising flour
2 tbsp clear honey
½ tsp bicarbonate of soda

Mix the sugar and soured cream or yoghurt together. Stir in the flour gradually and add the honey. Dissolve the bicarbonate of soda in a little water and stir into the cake; beat well for several minutes. Pour into a greased cake tin and bake at 180°C (350°F), Mark 4 for 40–45 minutes.

Scones *Makes about 16*

225g (8 oz) self-raising flour
pinch of salt

50g (2 oz) butter
125ml (¼ pt) milk or thin yoghurt, approx.

Sift the flour and salt into a bowl; rub in the butter. Add the milk and mix to a soft dough. Turn out onto a floured board and roll out to 1cm (½ in) thickness. Cut into rounds with a 5cm (2 in) biscuit cutter. Place on a greased baking tray and brush the tops with milk. Bake at 230°C (450°F), Mark 8 for 10 minutes until well risen and golden brown.

This is a basic mixture to which can be added sugar, dried fruit, spices or even cheese. Good wholemeal scones can be made with 225g (8 oz) wholemeal flour and 3 tsp baking powder with fresh milk or 1 tsp bicarbonate of soda with yoghurt.

Drop Scones *Makes about 24*

25g (1 oz) butter
25g (1 oz) sugar
225g (8 oz) plain flour
pinch of salt

1 tsp bicarbonate of soda
1 egg, beaten
250ml (½ pt) thin yoghurt or
 cultured buttermilk

Cream together the butter and sugar, add the flour, salt, bicarbonate of soda, the beaten egg and yoghurt to make a thick batter. Grease a frying pan and drop tablespoons of batter into the hot pan. Bake on each side until golden brown. Place in a clean teacloth to keep warm. Serve hot with butter and jam or honey.

Devon Flats *Makes about 20*

This is a traditional recipe.

150ml (¼ pt) clotted cream
225g (8 oz) self-raising flour
1 egg, beaten

100g (4 oz) sugar
a little milk

Rub the cream into the flour, add the beaten egg and sugar, and mix to a smooth dough with a little milk. Roll out on a floured board to ½cm (¼ in) thickness and cut into rounds with a 6cm (2½ in) biscuit cutter. Place on a greased baking tray, leaving room to spread and bake in a hot oven, 230°C (450°F), Mark 8 for 10 minutes.

Plain Dessert Biscuits *Makes several dozen biscuits*

This recipe is given by Eliza Acton. These excellent plain biscuits are ideal for accompanying cheese and wine and are very simple to make.

225g (8 oz) plain flour   25g (1 oz) butter
pinch of salt   150ml (¼ pt) milk

Sift the flour and salt together and rub in the butter. Make into a firm dough with the milk. Divide into 4 pieces and roll out each one very thinly, to paper thinness. Cut out with 5cm (2 in) biscuit cutter, prick them and place on a floured baking tray. Bake at 180°C (350°F), Mark 4 for 10–15 minutes. They should be very crisp and only slightly browned.

If slightly sweet biscuits are wanted add 25g (1 oz) icing sugar to the dough.

Wafers

Wafers were introduced by the Normans and were very popular in medieval times, and like the early 'cakes' they were eaten with wine or ale. The wafer-maker or waferer was a welcome street trader. Wafers were made in special round or square wafer irons, with long handles, so that they could be held over the fire. The incised designs on both sides of the iron became imprinted on the cooked wafers. The wafer irons were taken to America with the early settlers and now have come back to us as 'waffle irons'! Wafers were of various types, those made of a cream or milk batter were flat and crisp and slipped off the iron, those made from a stickier mixture had to be rolled off the iron onto an iron rod so that they were in a curled form similar to brandy snaps.

Dutch Wafers *Makes 6*

Given by Dorothy Hartley in *Food in England*, these wafers are made in a waffling iron.

125g (4 oz) plain flour   1 tsp sugar
pinch of salt   1 egg, beaten
7g (¼ oz) fresh yeast or 1 tsp dried yeast   50g (2 oz) melted butter
150ml (¼ pt) warm milk   1 tsp rosewater (optional)

Sift the flour and salt into a bowl. Cream or dissolve the yeast with a little warm milk and the sugar. Make a well in the flour and pour in the yeast, beaten egg, melted butter, rosewater and the rest of the milk. Beat well to make a pouring batter. Leave to rise for 1 hour. Heat and grease the waffle iron and pour in the batter to spread over the iron and close. Cook on a low heat until the mixture swells and sets and the underside is brown. Turn over and cook on the other side. When cooked the wafer will separate from the iron and can be tipped out. Grease the iron between cooking each wafer. Serve hot with wine sauce (see p. 37), golden syrup, or a hot jam sauce and double cream.

Brown Wafers *Makes several dozen*

Hannah Glasse's recipe.

75g (3 oz) flour   1 egg yolk
pinch of salt   150ml (¼ pt) single cream
50g (2 oz) sugar   ½ tsp cinnamon

Sift the flour and the salt, mix in the sugar. Make a well in the centre and put in the egg yolk and the cream. Beat to a smooth batter and add the cinnamon. Put teaspoonfuls of batter on a hot greased baking tray, leaving room to spread, and bake at 180°C (350°F), Mark 4 for 10 minutes until golden brown. They should be very thin and crisp. Store in an airtight tin. Serve with ice cream, cream desserts and junket.

Wafers *Makes 12*

Elizabeth Raffald's recipe.

2 tbsp flour   2 tbsp single cream
2 tbsp sugar   1 tbsp orange flower water or orange juice

Beat the ingredients together very well, Elizabeth Raffald suggests for 30 minutes! Drop teaspoons of the mixture onto a well buttered baking tray, leaving plenty of room for spreading. Bake at 180°C (350°F), Mark 4 for about 7 minutes until they turn golden brown all over. Remove from the oven, lift off and roll round the handle of a wooden spoon quickly. Leave until firm and slide off the handle. Serve with ice cream, syllabubs and possets.

Cheesecakes

Cheesecakes come in many shapes and guises: hot or cold, cooked or uncooked, with a sharp cheese flavour or none at all. Many of the cheesecakes so popular now are of European or American origin, usually with a biscuit crumb base, a rich cream cheese filling and a fruit sauce topping. Traditional English cheesecakes are milder in flavour and are made from fresh curds, or often other ingredients not at all related to cheese. Medieval cheese tarts were in fact made from a mature cheese which had to be pounded to a paste in a mortar first and then mixed with egg yolks, sugar and spices to make the tart filling. It was later that fresh curds became the basis of the filling together with eggs, spices and dried fruit. Cheesecakes were also made from egg custard mixed with rice or bread, and spices.

Maids of Honour *Makes 12*

It is said that these were invented at Richmond for Elizabeth I, and her ladies-in-waiting so liked them that the cakes took their name.

puff or shortcrust pastry
  or cream crust
  using 100g (4 oz) flour
  (see Appendix 1 and Cheese Puffs, p. 61)
125g (4 oz) fresh curds
50g (2 oz) butter

2 eggs
1 tbsp brandy or sherry
50g (2 oz) ground almonds
50g (2 oz) sugar
grated rind and juice of
  1 lemon

Line patty or tartlet tins with the pastry. Beat the curds with the butter. Whisk the eggs with brandy until frothy and add to the curds with the ground almonds, sugar, lemon juice and rind. Place the mixture in the pastry cases. Bake at 180°C (350°F), Mark 4 for 20 minutes.

Fine Cheesecake *Serves 4*

Given by Hannah Glasse.

shortcrust pastry using 100g (4 oz) flour
  (see Appendix 1)
225g (8 oz) fresh curds
2 tbsp single cream
75g (3 oz) macaroon crumbs

1 egg, beaten
½ tsp nutmeg
1 tsp rosewater (optional)
150ml (¼ pt) soured cream
  (optional)

Line an 18cm (7 in) flan tin with the pastry. Beat the curds with the cream, then beat in the egg. Stir in the macaroon crumbs, nutmeg and rosewater. Put the mixture into the pastry case and bake at 180°C (350°F), Mark 4 for 30–40 minutes. Serve hot or cold. If liked, a soured cream topping can be put on this. Pour over cooked filling and return to the oven for 5 minutes.

Italian Cheesecake *Serves 4*

Robert May's recipe.

shortcrust pastry using 100g (4 oz)
  flour (see Appendix 1)
125g (4 oz) fresh curds

125g (4 oz) Cheddar cheese, grated
50g (2 oz) sugar
50g (2 oz) currants

2 tbsp single cream
1 egg, beaten

½ tsp cinnamon
½ tsp nutmeg

Line an 18cm (7 in) flan tin with the pastry. Beat the curds with the cream and the egg. Stir in the Cheddar cheese, sugar, currants, cinnamon and nutmeg. Put the mixture into the pastry case and bake at 180°C (350°F), Mark 4 for 30–40 minutes.

Yorkshire Curd Cheesecake *Serves 4–6*

A traditional recipe.

shortcrust pastry using 150g (6 oz) flour (see Appendix 1)
225g (8 oz) acid curd or cream cheese
50g (2 oz) melted butter

50g (2 oz) sugar
1 egg, beaten
grated rind of ½ lemon
½ tsp nutmeg
50g (2 oz) currants

Line a 20cm (8 in) flan tin with the pastry, saving a little for a lattice work top. Beat the cheese with the butter, sugar, egg, lemon rind and nutmeg. Stir in the currants. Put the mixture in the pastry case and finish with a lattice work of pastry on top. Brush with a little beaten egg or milk and bake at 180°C (350°F), Mark 4 for 40–45 minutes until lightly browned.

Blackcherry Cheesecake *Serves 6*

Base:
100g (4 oz) digestive biscuits
50g (2 oz) melted butter

25g (1 oz) caster sugar
½ tsp cinnamon

Filling:
225g (8 oz) acid curd or cream cheese
2 eggs, separated
50g (2 oz) sugar

1 tbsp cornflour
grated rind of ½ lemon
2 tbsp cream

Topping:
250g (8 oz) black cherries, fresh or tinned

50g (2 oz) sugar
2 tsp arrowroot

Crush the biscuits. Mix with the melted butter, sugar and cinnamon. Place this mixture in the base of an 18–20cm (7–8 in) greased loose-bottomed cake tin and press down evenly. Beat the cheese. Mix together the egg yolks, sugar, cornflour, lemon rind and cream and add to the cheese. Whisk the egg whites until lightly stiff. Carefully fold into the cheese mixture. Pour into the cake tin and bake at 150°C (300°F), Mark 2 for 45 minutes. Turn off the heat and open the oven door, leave to cool slowly in the oven for 30 minutes. Cool in the tin and remove carefully. If fresh cherries are used bring to the boil with 4 tbsp water and the sugar and cook for a few minutes. Drain off the juice into another pan; remove the cherry stones and chop the cherries roughly. The tinned cherries will not need cooking. Mix the arrowroot with the cooking juice or 4 tbsp can juice and bring to the boil stirring all the time. Add the fruit and cool. Pour over the cheesecake. Chill.

Other fruit can be used for the topping: black or redcurrants, or blackberries. For a quick topping a jam sauce can be used. Dilute 4 heaped tbsp jam of your choice with a little water, add the arrowroot and boil to thicken.

Chilled Cheesecake *Serves 4*

50g (2 oz) digestive biscuits   2 eggs, separated
1 tbsp golden syrup   50g (2 oz) sugar
25g (1 oz) melted butter   grated rind of ½ lemon
15g (½ oz) gelatine   225g (8 oz) acid curd or cream cheese

To decorate: chopped nuts, fresh fruit, whipped cream

Grease a 15–18cm (6–7 in) loose-bottomed cake tin. Crush biscuits and mix with the melted butter and syrup. Press into the cake tin, and chill until firm. Dissolve the gelatine in 3 tbsp hot water (see Appendix 1). Beat the egg yolks, sugar and lemon rind over hot water until the mixture begins to thicken. Remove from the heat and stir in the gelatine. Cool but do not allow to set. Stir into the beaten cheese. Beat the egg whites until stiff and fold into the cheese mixture. Pour into the cake tin and leave to set. Remove from tin and lift off the base. Decorate with chopped nuts, and whipped cream or fresh fruit.

12 Drinks

Milk was not as popular as a straight drink on its own as it is today, although the by-products of butter and cheesemaking, buttermilk and whey were drunk by poor countryfolk through the ages. Buttermilk as a drink was probably consumed most often in its sour state, so that it was slightly thickened. If you make butter, you can drink your own buttermilk, either sweet, or sour if you make cultured buttermilk. It always tastes better well chilled. Otherwise yoghurt can form our modern equivalent of the sour buttermilk. In the sixteenth and seventeenth centuries whey became a fashionable drink for the upper and middle classes as well since it was thought to have beneficial medicinal properties. Whey houses were opened in London, which proved to be good meeting places for townspeople, and whey and buttermilk could also be bought in the streets. A variety of whey drinks were produced: the milk could be curdled with red or white wine, citrus fruits and even scurvy-grass juice or cream of tartar.

Hot posset described by Dr Johnson as 'milk curdled with wine and other acids' was made in various forms from medieval times. Simple possets were made from milk and ale, perhaps thickened with breadcrumbs, while thicker mixtures were made from cream and sack (a form of sherry) or brandy, eggs, sugar and spices and thickened with crushed biscuits. In many ways they resembled the syllabubs with the addition of eggs or breadcrumbs to thicken. They were drunk (or eaten) on festive occasions from special cups, and also were considered a nutritious and digestible food for convalescents. Punch was an old Indian drink, its name coming from the hindu word for 'five' referring to its ingredients: sugar, citrus juices, spirits, water and spices. It was introduced by the East India merchants and later a milk punch became popular, served in a bowl with toast or biscuits floating on the top.

Tea, coffee and chocolate all arrived in England in the mid-seventeenth century and very soon became popular drinks. Chocolate and coffee houses sprang up at this time too. Drinking chocolate or coffee were taken with wiggs or toast and butter as a light breakfast by the rich and middle classes. At first chocolate was made with wine, but it was not long before milk was used. Later milk was added to tea and coffee. Eventually tea became the national drink consumed by all classes, drunk with sugar and milk. In fact today most of the milk consumed in this country is taken in tea.

As well as old and traditional milk drinks, I have included some modern.

White Wine Whey *Serves 2–3*

Dr Kitchener's recipe.

600ml (1 pt) milk   sugar
1–2 glasses white wine

Boil the milk and add the wine. Heat again to boiling point and leave to stand. Leave to settle, then strain through butter muslin of double thickness. Sweeten to taste and chill. Save the curd to use in cheesecakes.

Milk Lemonade *Serves 4–5*

Eliza Acton's recipe.

175g (6 oz) sugar	150ml (¼ pt) sherry
600ml (1 pt) water	450ml (¾ pt) milk
150ml (¼ pt) lemon juice	

Dissolve the sugar in boiling water, add the lemon juice, sherry and milk. Leave to settle, then strain through butter muslin of double thickness. Chill before serving. Save the curd to use in cheesecakes.

Ale Posset *Serves 4*

Eighteenth century recipe.

600ml (1 pt) light ale	600ml (1 pt) milk
½ tsp nutmeg	25g (1 oz) breadcrumbs
50g (2 oz) sugar	

Heat the beer with the nutmeg and sugar and put into a glass bowl. Pour the milk on top of the breadcrumbs and heat. When the milk boils, pour it into the beer, and serve.

Sack Posset *Serves 2–3*

Elizabeth Raffald's recipe.

25g (1 oz) sponge biscuit crumbs (see Appendix 1)	150–300ml (¼–½ pt) sherry slice of lemon
600ml (1 pt) single cream or milk	50g (2 oz) sugar
1 small piece of cinnamon	

Add the biscuit crumbs to the cream with the cinnamon. Boil until thick. Remove the cinnamon stick and add the sherry, slice of lemon, and sugar and heat gently without boiling. Serve with dry toast.

Oatmeal Posset *Serves 2–3*

A traditional Scottish recipe.

3 tbsp oatmeal flour	4 tbsp sherry
600ml (1 pt) milk	4 tbsp light ale
½ tsp nutmeg	50g (2 oz) sugar (optional)
½ tsp cinnamon	

Mix the oatmeal with the milk, nutmeg and cinnamon. Bring to the boil and simmer until it thickens. Heat the sherry, light ale and sugar and add to the milk and oatmeal. Simmer for a few minutes. Serve in a warm bowl.

Cambridge Milk Punch *Serves 2–3*

Eliza Acton's recipe.

600ml (1 pt) milk	1 egg yolk beaten with 2 tbsp milk
grated rind of ½ lemon	150ml (¼ pt) rum
50g (2 oz) sugar	4 tbsp brandy

Heat the milk, lemon rind and sugar. Strain and pour over the beaten egg yolk. Return to a low heat and add the rum and brandy gradually. Remove from the heat, whisk to a froth and serve immediately in warm glasses, with Wafers (see p. 107) or Plain Dessert Biscuits (see p. 106).

Auld Man's Milk *Serves 3–4*

A traditional Scottish recipe.

2 eggs, separated	150ml (¼ pt) rum, whisky or
50g (2 oz) sugar	brandy
600ml (1 pt) milk	nutmeg

Beat the egg yolks and sugar together until thick and pale yellow in colour. Bring the milk to the boil and beat into the egg yolks with the rum. Beat the egg whites until stiff and fold into the mixture gently. Pour into a glass bowl or individual glasses, sprinkle with nutmeg and serve immediately.

Ozyat *Serves 2–3*

Elizabeth Raffald's recipe, this is an almond-flavoured milk drink which came to England from France in the seventeenth century.

600ml (1 pt) milk	½ tsp almond essence
1 small piece of cinnamon	1 tsp rosewater
50g (2 oz) ground almonds	50g (2 oz) sugar

Boil the milk with the other ingredients, then strain through butter muslin. Chill and serve cold.

Yoghurt Drink *Serves 2–3*

300ml (½ pt) yoghurt	1 tbsp chopped mint
300ml (½ pt) cold water	salt or sugar to taste

Beat the yoghurt, and then beat in the water gradually until they are well blended together. A liquidizer can be used. Add the chopped mint, and salt or sugar according to your own taste. Serve well chilled.

Fruit and Yoghurt Cup *Serves 2–3*

300ml (½ pt) yoghurt or cultured buttermilk   sugar to taste
300ml (½ pt) fruit juice: lemon, orange or pineapple

Blend or whisk the yoghurt or buttermilk and fruit juice together. Add sugar to taste and serve well chilled. A slice of orange can be slit and slipped over the rim of the glasses if liked.

Iced Coffee *Serves 3–4*

300ml (½ pt) strong black coffee   sugar to taste
300ml (½ pt) milk or single cream   crushed ice

Blend or whisk the coffee with the milk or cream. Add sugar to taste. Chill well. Put a little crushed ice in the base of the serving glasses and pour iced coffee on top.

Chocolate Milk Shake *Serves 4*

2 tbsp cocoa   50g (2 oz) sugar
2 tbsp boiling water   1 tsp vanilla essence
900ml (1½ pt) milk   4 tbsp vanilla ice cream (optional)

Mix the cocoa with the boiling water to a smooth paste. Whisk or blend with the milk, sugar, vanilla essence and ice cream. Pour into glasses and serve immediately.

Fruit Milk Shake *Serves 4*

150ml (¼ pt) fruit purée (Strawberry,   600ml (1 pt) milk
  raspberry, apricot, banana,   sugar to taste, according to fruit
  blackcurrant or blackberry purée   4 tbsp vanilla ice cream
  from fresh, frozen or tinned fruit)   or 4 tbsp crushed ice

Whisk or blend all the ingredients together. Pour into glasses and serve immediately.

Chilled Orange Posset *Serves 2–3*

600ml (1 pt) milk   150ml (¼ pt) orange juice
2 eggs, beaten   2 tbsp sherry or brandy (optional)
50g (2 oz) sugar   crushed ice

Heat the milk and pour over the beaten eggs with the sugar. Return to heat and heat gently until the mixture thickens slightly. Chill thoroughly. Whisk or blend in orange juice, sherry or brandy and crushed ice. Pour into glasses and serve.

Appendix 1

Culinary notes

Weights and measures

Metric and imperial measurements are shown throughout. The metric quantities are not exact conversions but in each recipe are calculated so that proportions of the ingredients are right, to give good results.

Spoon measures are level spoons; a level teaspoon (tsp) is 5ml and a level tablespoon (tbsp) is 15ml.

Ingredients and cooking methods

Flour, Sugar and Eggs

Unless otherwise stated, use white, plain or self-raising flour, white granulated or caster sugar and size 3 or 4 (standard) eggs.

Rosewater

The distilled water from rose petals was much used for flavouring in sixteenth and seventeenth century cookery, and was also added to medicinal potions and cosmetics. It will be found as an optional ingredient in some of the recipes and is easily and cheaply available from most chemists.

Orange Flower Water

Orange flower water was another popular flavouring agent, but unlike the home-produced rosewater it had to be imported. It too can be obtained from most chemists.

Sponge Biscuits *Makes 12*

Trifles and some of the hot puddings call for sponge biscuits. Here is an easy recipe to make at home.

40g (1½ oz) plain flour   40g (1½ oz) sugar
pinch of salt   a little grated lemon
1 egg, separated   rind (optional)

Sift together the flour and salt. Beat the egg white stiffly, add the sugar and beat again. Stir in the beaten egg yolk and fold in the flour and lemon rind. Pipe or spoon the mixture onto a greased baking tray in 7½cm (3 in) lengths. Dust with caster sugar. Bake at 180°C (350°F), Mark 4 for about 10 minutes.

Macaroons *Makes 18*

These are relatively expensive to buy, and can be made easily at home. You can employ the spare egg whites to make macaroons after having used the yolks for other recipes. They will keep well in an airtight tin.

rice paper
2 egg whites
100g (4 oz) ground almonds
200g (8 oz) caster sugar
25g (1 oz) ground rice
½ tsp vanilla essence
½ tsp almond essence

Well butter a baking tray and line with rice paper. Beat the egg whites until foamy but not stiff. Add almonds, sugar, ground rice, the vanilla and almond essence and beat well. Pipe or spoon heaps of the mixture onto the rice paper, leaving room for the macaroons to spread. Bake at 160°C (325°F), Mark 3 for 20–25 minutes until pale brown. Remove from the oven, leave for a few minutes, then lift off, tearing away the rice paper from around the edges of each.

Croûtons

These are a good accompaniment to soups and other dishes. Cut stale bread into cubes, square or triangular shapes and fry in clarified butter until golden brown. Drain well on kitchen paper and keep hot and crisp until required. Alternatively, thick slices of bread can be buttered, then cut into cubes and baked on a baking tray, butterside down, at 180°C (350°F), Mark 4 until golden.

Shortcrust Pastry

The pies and tarts use shortcrust pastry. You can of course use your favourite recipe, but I give one below.

100g (4 oz) flour   50g (2 oz) butter
pinch of salt   cold water to mix

Sift together the flour and salt. Rub in the butter so that the mixture looks like fine breadcrumbs. Add just enough water to make a stiff dough. Knead into a smooth ball, leaving the sides of the bowl clean. Place on a floured board and roll out as required.

For recipes requiring shortcrust pastry with 150g (6 oz) flour, use 75g (3 oz) butter; for 75g (3 oz) flour use 40g (1½ oz) butter.

To Bake Blind

Cooked but empty pastry cases are often

required, to be filled later. To bake blind, first line the flan tin with pastry, then line the pastry with aluminium foil which will prevent the pastry rising as it cooks. Bake at 200°C (400°F), Mark 6 for 15 minutes. Remove from oven and take off foil.

To Dissolve Gelatine

Many of the recipes use gelatine. To dissolve the gelatine, sprinkle into a cup containing the hot water and stir. To make sure it fully dissolves, stand the cup in a saucepan of hot water over a low heat and stir.

Appendix 2
The cookery writers

The recipes in this book come from many sources and the full list is given in the bibliography. Some of the old cookery books and writers are particularly worthy of special note.

Forme of Cury   This manuscript was compiled by the cooks of Richard II and was written about 1390. The original roll is in the British Museum, as is also a reproduction made in the eighteenth century by Dr Samuel Pegge.

Two Fifteenth Century Cookery Books Harleian Miscellany 279 and 4016.
These were collected by the Early English Text Society in 1888, and provide an illuminating insight into medieval meals and recipes. They can be seen in the British Museum and other good libraries.

Robert May (1588–?)
The Accomplisht Cook, 1671. Robert May was a professional cook and son of a professional cook, but undoubtably well educated for a man of his time. He spent part of his early life in Paris, was apprenticed in London and then served in the large country houses of the gentry.

Hannah Glasse (1708–1770)
The Art of Cookery made Plain and Easy, 1747. Hannah Glasse's cookery book was a best seller for a hundred years and ran to many editions. She married young, had 8 children,

4 of whom died and was a habit maker to the court by profession. She was very disparaging about French cooks, and preferred good, simple English dishes.

Elizabeth Raffald (1731–1781)
The Experienced English Housekeeper, 1769. Elizabeth Raffald was a remarkable woman for her time and what she achieved in her life would show up many 'liberated' women of today. She worked as a housekeeper for 15 years and then at 30 married John Raffald. He proved to be lazy and unsuccessful in his business so that Elizabeth herself had to support her increasing family; she had 15 daughters in 18 years and finally died in childbirth. During these 18 years she opened cook and confectionery shops selling prepared dishes, founded the first servants' employment agency, managed two well-known inns, issued the first street and trade directory in Manchester, launched a cookery school for young ladies, influenced the publication of two newspapers, and wrote her famous book.

Dr William Kitchener (1775–1827)
The Cook's Oracle, 1817. Dr Kitchener was a member of the intelligentsia of his day; after obtaining a Scottish medical degree which was not recognized in England, he dabbled in various arts and sciences, in optics, in music and in cookery. He wrote books on telescopes and spectacles, composed operettas as well as writing *The Cook's Oracle*.

Eliza Acton (1799–1859)
Modern Cookery for Private Families, 1845. Eliza Acton was first known as a poet but after a book of verse was turned down by her publishers they suggested she write a cookery book instead. She was able to turn her talents to this subject with ease and her very practical book was immediately successful.

Isabella Beeton (1836–1865)
The Book of Household Mangement, 1861. Isabella Beeton is perhaps the most famous of all cookery writers. She was another one who had to support an improvident husband. Her husband, Samuel, was a publisher and the success of his periodical, "The Englishwoman's Domestic Magazine", was largely due to Isabella's efforts. *The Book of*

Household Management was first published in this magazine in monthly parts, and then later as a complete book. It makes fascinating reading, not only the cookery section which is filled with anecdotes on the origins of ingredients and botanical and zoological detail, but also the sections dealing with servants, child rearing, illness and legal memoranda. It is remarkable that this was written by a young woman in her early twenties; she died when only 29.

I also found invaluable Dorothy Hartley's *Food in England* and Anne Wilson's *Food and Drink in Britain* which are modern surveys of English food and drink, meals and eating habits through the ages. Both are treasure-troves of information and are illustrated with reproductions of old plates. The former has in addition beautiful line drawings throughout to illustrate the text.

Bibliography

Acton, E., *Modern Cookery for Private Families*, 1845, reprinted by Elek Books, 1966

Allison, S., *The Dairy Book of Home Cookery*, Milk Marketing Board, 1978

Austin, T., ed., *Two Fifteenth-Century Cookery Books*: Harleian MS 279 and 4016, Early English Text Society, 1888

Aylett, M., and Ordish, O., *First Catch Your Hare*, MacDonald, 1965

Ayrton, E., *The Cookery of England*, Penguin Books, 1977

Beeton, I., *The Book of Household Management*, 1861, reprinted by Cape, 1968

Burnett, J., *Plenty and Want*, Nelson, 1966

Carter, C., *The Complete Practical Cook*, 1730

Cheke, V., *The Story of Cheesemaking in Britain*, Routledge and Kegan Paul, 1959

de Gouy, L., *Icecream and Icecream Desserts*, Constable, 1966

Drummond, J. C., and Wilbraham, A., *The Englishman's Food*, Cape, 1939

Edden, H., *County Recipes of Old England*, Country Life, 1929

Farley, J., *The London Art of Cookery*, 1783

Farmhouse Fare, Countrywise Books, 1973

The Forme of Cury, in *Antiquitates Culinariae*, ed., R. Warner, 1791

Fowler, B., and Rosenbaum, E., *The Roman Cookery Book, a critical translation of the art of cooking*, Harrap, 1958. Based on Apicius

Frond, N., *The World Book of Soups*, Pelham Books, 1972.

Fussell, G., *The English Dairy Farmer 1500–1900*, Frank Cass, 1966

Glasse, H., *The Art of Cookery Made Plain and Easy*, 1747; 1796 edition reprinted by S. R. Publishers, 1971

Grigson, J., *English Food*, Macmillan, 1974

Grimley, G., ed., *The Victorian Cookery Book*, Abelard-Schuman, 1973

Mrs Groundes-Peaces Old Cookery Notebook, International Wine and Food Publ. Co., David and Charles, 1971

Hartley, D., *Food in England*, MacDonald, 1954

Heaton, N., *Traditional Recipes of the British Isles*, Faber, 1951

Kitchener, W. *Apicius Redivivus, The Cook's Oracle*, 1822

Mabey, R., *Food for Free*, Collins, 1972

Markham, G., *The English Huswife*, 1615

May, R., *The Accomplisht Cook*, 1671

McKendry, M., *Seven Centuries of English Cooking*, Weidenfield and Nicolson, 1973

Nilson, B., *Cooking with Yogurt, Cultured Cream and Soft Cheese*, Pelham Books, 1973

Nilson, B., *Making Ice Cream and Cold Sweets*, Pelham Books, 1973

Partridge, J., *The Treasurie of Hidden Secrets*, 1653

Pearse, M., *Traditional British Cookery*, International Wine and Food Publ. Co., David and Charles, 1972

Platt, Sir Hugh, *Delightes for Ladies*, 1552–1611, with introduction by G. E. Fussell and K. R. Fussell, Crosby, Lockwood and Son, 1948

Price, Rebecca, *The Compleat Cook or the Secrets of a Seventeenth Century Housewife*, Introduced by Madeleine Masson, Routledge and Kegan Paul, 1974

Pullar, P., *Consuming Passions*, Hamish Hamilton, 1970

Raffald, E., *The Experienced English Housekeeper*, 1769, reprinted by E. & W. Books, 1970

White, F., *Good Things in England*, Cape, 1932

Wilson, C. A., *Food and Drink in Britain*, Constable, 1973

Index